TEACHER'S GUIDE

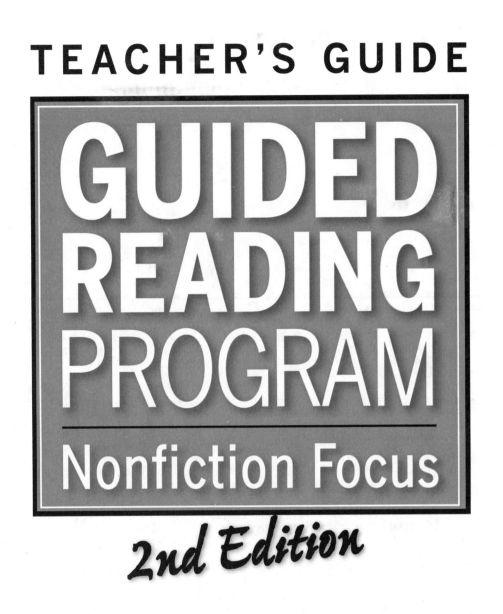

GUIDED READING PROGRAM

Nonfiction Focus

2nd Edition

Book cover credits (page 135): *Wonderstruck* by Brian Selznick. Copyright © 2011 by Brian Selznick. Published by Scholastic Inc. *Titanic Sinks!* by Barry Denenberg. Text copyright © 2011 by Barry Denenberg. Published by Scholastic Inc. by arrangement with Penguin Group (USA) Inc. Cover: National Museums Northern Ireland, 2011, Ulster Folk & Transport Museum. *What Do Roots Do?* by Kathleen V. Kudlinski, illustrated by David Schuppert. Text copyright © 2005 by Kathleen V. Kudlinski. Illustrations copyright © 2005 by David Schuppert. Published by Scholastic Inc. by arrangement with The Rowman & Littlefield Publishing Group. *Elephants* by Kate Riggs. Copyright © 2011 by Creative Paperbacks. Published by Scholastic Inc. by arrangement with The Creative Company. *Detector Dogs* by Judith Bauer Stamper. Copyright © 2014 by Scholastic Inc. Published by Scholastic Inc. Cover: K9 Storm Incorporated. *Gettysburg: The Graphic Novel* by C. M. Butzer. Copyright © 2009 by C. M. Butzer. Published by Scholastic Inc. by arrangement with HarperCollins Children's Books. *Jackie Robinson: American Hero* by Sharon Robinson. Copyright © 2013 by Sharon Robinson. Published by Scholastic Inc. Cover fg: Bettmann/Corbis, bg: Randy Faris/Corbis. *Blackout* by John Rocco. Copyright © 2011 by John Rocco. Published by Scholastic Inc. by arrangement with Hyperion Books for Children. *Sounds on the Farm* by Alex Ives. Copyright © 2014 by Scholastic Inc. Published by Scholastic Inc. Cover t: Ronald van der Beek/Shutterstock, c: janecat/Shutterstock, b: Tristan Tan/Shutterstock. *Biblioburro* by Jeanette Winter. Copyright © 2010 by Jeanette Winter. Published by Scholastic Inc. by arrangement with Simon & Schuster Children's Publishing Division. *Playing to Win* by Karen Deans, illustrated by Elbrite Brown. Text copyright © 2007 by Karen Deans. Illustrations copyright © 2007 by Elbrite Brown. Published by Scholastic Inc. by arrangement with Holiday House, Inc.

Common Core State Standards copyright © 2010 National Governors Association Center for Best Practices, Council of Chief State School Officers. All rights reserved.

Portions previously published in *Guided Reading Program: Text Types Teacher's Guide*, copyright © 2011.

ISBN-13: 978-0-545-64755-7
ISBN-10: 0-545-64755-X

Table of Contents

Table of Contents (continued)

Using the Guided Reading Program

USING YOUR
GUIDED READING PROGRAM

The Scholastic Guided Reading Program is a varied collection of books that are categorized by the kind and level of challenge they offer children as they are learning to read. The Guided Reading Program consists of 260 books organized into 26 levels of difficulty—Levels A–Z. Many different characteristics of the texts are considered in determining the level of challenge and support a particular book or shorter story presents.

Advantages of a Leveled Book Collection

A leveled book set has many advantages, including the following:

- **It provides experience with a wide variety of texts within a level.**
- **It facilitates the process of selecting books for groups of children.**
- **It lends itself to flexible grouping.**
- **It provides a way to assess children's progress.**
- **It provides a basic book collection that can be expanded over time.**

Multiple Copies of Books	Six copies of each book are provided so that children in small groups will have access to their own copies. Having a collection of books on various levels, with multiple copies of each book, allows you to consider individual strengths when grouping and selecting books. To help you quickly identify a book's level, you may wish to place a Guided Reading Program sticker for the level on the front or back of each book cover.
Flexibility of Use	With a gradient of text, grouping can be more flexible. Children might read only some of the books in a level, and not necessarily in the same sequence. In addition, children may change groups based on individual needs. The **Characteristics of Text** and **Behaviors to Notice and Support** on pages 94–119 will assist you in placing children in the appropriate levels.
	If you note that some students need extra support for a particular text or that the selection is too difficult for most of the group, you can abandon guided reading and instead use shared reading to experience the book. Then you can select an easier book the next day. As students progress, have them reread books on a lower level for enjoyment. Students will become more confident readers as they reread a book for meaning with no need for problem solving.
Adding to the Guided Reading Program	The Guided Reading Program has been designed with adaptability in mind, so you may add copies of children's and your own favorite books to the library. You may place a Guided Reading Program sticker for the suggested level on each book you add.

Variety Within Levels in the Collection

When working with groups in classroom reading, a broad base of text is needed. The Guided Reading Program provides this broad base. Readers who experience only one kind of book may develop a narrow range of strategies for processing text. With a leveled set, difficulty is controlled because all text characteristics have been factored in. Yet the level of text is not artificially controlled because the variety of text characteristics occurs within natural story language.

The early levels of the Guided Reading Program introduce students to reading print. While reading at these beginning levels, students apply phonics skills, develop a core of high-frequency words, work with print in a variety of layouts, and engage with a variety of high-interest texts.

Books at later levels (Levels J and beyond) include a wider range of text. Within each level, literary texts are included. Essentially, there are three kinds of books at these levels, although there is variety within each category.

- **First, there are informational books that have photographs and are generally shorter. These present complex ideas and some technical language. They challenge students to acquire and discuss ideas, information, and points of view (argument writing) that go beyond the text and to research topics that are of interest to them.**

- **Second, there are picture books that offer informational text at a more sophisticated level than ever before. These picture books provide an opportunity to expand vocabulary and to recognize how illustrations and photos contribute information. Like the short story, picture books provide the advanced reader with complex reading material that does not take several days to complete.**

- **Third, there are longer chapter books, plays, and graphic novels. These longer selections provide an opportunity for readers to sustain reading over time, remembering details and information and, in fiction selections, getting to know characters as they develop.**

FACTORS CONSIDERED IN
LEVELING BOOKS

In placing a book, short story, or article along a gradient of text, multiple characteristics of text are considered. Here is a sample list.

Book and Print Features
Refers to the physical aspects of the text—what readers cope with in terms of length, size, print layout, and font size. It also refers to the interpretation of illustrations and the relationships between information in graphics and the body of the text.

- How many words are in the book?
- How many lines of text are on each page?
- How many pages are in the book?
- What size is the print?
- How much space is there between words and lines?
- How easy is it to find information?
- What is the relationship between print and illustrations?
- Are there graphics (photos, diagrams, maps) that provide essential information, and how easy are the graphics to interpret?
- What are the features of the print layout? (For example, do sentences begin on the left or do they "wrap around" so that end punctuation must be relied upon?)
- Is print placed in standard, predictable places on the pages or is it used in creative ways that require the reader's flexibility?
- Do the size and shape of book, binding, and layout play a role in text interpretation?

Genre
Means the "type" or "kind" and refers to a classification system formed to provide a way of talking about what texts are like (fiction—including realistic fiction, fantasy, traditional literature; and nonfiction/informational text—including biography and autobiography).

- What is the "genre" or "kind" of book?
- What special demands does this genre make on readers?
- Is this an easy or more difficult example of the genre?

Content
Refers to the subject matter that readers are required to understand as they read both fiction and nonfiction texts.

- What background information is essential for understanding this text?
- What new information will readers need to grasp the text?
- How accessible to the reader is the content?

Themes and Ideas
Refers to the "big picture," the universality of the problem in the text and its relevance to people's lives.

- What is the theme of the text?
- Are there multiple themes that the reader must understand and be able to talk about?
- How accessible to the reader are the "big ideas"?

Language and Literary Features

Refers to the writer's style and use of literary devices. Literary features are those elements typically used in literature to capture imagination, stir emotions, create empathy or suspense, give readers a sense that the characters and story are real, and make readers care about the outcome of the plot. Informational texts may incorporate some literary features.

- From what perspective is the story or informational text written?
- Does the book include devices such as headings, labels, and captions?
- Are graphical elements such as diagrams, tables, charts, and maps included?
- To what degree does the writer use literary language, such as metaphor?
- How easy is it to understand the characters and their motivations and development?
- Is character development essential to the story?
- Is dialogue assigned (using *he said*) or unassigned with longer stretches of interchange that the reader must follow and attribute to one character or another?
- How are characters revealed through what they say or think and what others say or think about them?
- How essential to the story are understandings about setting and plot?

Vocabulary and Words

Refers to the words and their accessibility to readers. Vocabulary generally refers to the meaning of words that readers may decode but not understand. Word solving refers to both decoding and to understanding meaning.

- What is the frequency of multisyllabic words in the text?
- How complex are word meanings? (For example, are readers required to understand multiple meanings or subtle shades of meaning of words?)
- What prior knowledge is needed to understand the vocabulary of the text?
- How many content or technical words are included in the text? How complex are these words?
- Does informational text utilize timeless verb constructions? (Ants *carry* sand as opposed to *carried*.)
- Are generic noun constructions used in informational and/or nonfiction text?

Sentence Complexity

Refers to the syntactic patterns readers will encounter in the text; sentences may be simple (short, with one subject and predicate) or complex (longer, with embedded clauses).

- What is the average length of sentences in the text?
- To what degree do sentences contain embedded clauses?
- What is the sentence style of the writer?
- Are there complex sentences joined by *and, but,* or other conjunctions?
- Are paragraphs organized so that readers can recognize lead sentences and main ideas?

Punctuation

Refers to the graphic symbols that signal the way text should be read to reflect the author's meaning.

- What punctuation symbols are used in the text?
- What do readers need to notice about punctuation in order to fully understand the text?
- What punctuation is essential for readers to notice to read with fluency and phrasing?

Using Leveled Books With Readers

The success of guided reading depends on many factors other than text characteristics. These, of course, have to do with the young readers using the texts as well as teacher-student interactions and include:

- **The reader's prior knowledge of the topic, including vocabulary and concepts**
- **The reader's prior experience with texts that have similar features**
- **The way the teacher introduces the text**
- **The supportive interactions between the teacher and students before, during, and after reading**
- **The level of interest teachers help students build**

Level-by-Level Descriptions

Characteristics of text for each level in the Guided Reading Program are listed on pages 94–119. These descriptions are general: not every book included in a level will have every characteristic noted. Also listed are some important behaviors to notice and support at each level. As you use these books with students, you will notice how they support and challenge readers.

Other Resources

You may want to refer to the following resources for descriptions of guided reading as well as additional books for each level:

- Duke, Nell K., and Bennett-Armistead, V. Susan, 2003. *Reading & Writing Informational Text in the Primary Grades*. New York, NY: Scholastic Inc.
- Fountas, I. C., and Pinnell, G. S., 2008. *Benchmark Assessment System 1 and 2*. Portsmouth, NH: Heinemann.
- Fountas, I. C., and Pinnell, G. S., 1996. *Guided Reading: Good First Teaching for All Children*. Portsmouth, NH: Heinemann.
- Fountas, I. C., and Pinnell, G. S., 2001. *Guiding Readers and Writers, Grades 3–6: Teaching Comprehension, Genre, and Content Literacy*. Portsmouth, NH: Heinemann.
- Fountas, I. C., and Pinnell, G. S., 2005. *Leveled Books, K–8: Matching Texts to Readers for Effective Teaching*. Portsmouth, NH: Heinemann.
- Fountas, I. C., and Pinnell, G. S., 1999. *Voices on Word Matters*. Portsmouth, NH: Heinemann.
- Pinnell, G. S., and Fountas, I. C., 2007. *The Continuum of Literacy Learning, Grades K–8: Behaviors and Understandings to Notice, Teach, and Support*. Portsmouth, NH: Heinemann.
- Pinnell, G. S., and Fountas, I. C., 1998. *Word Matters: Teaching Phonics and Spelling in the Reading/Writing Classroom*. Portsmouth, NH: Heinemann.
- Fountas, I. C., and Pinnell, G. S., 2006. *Teaching for Comprehending and Fluency: Thinking, Talking, and Writing About Reading, K–8*. Portsmouth, NH: Heinemann.

WHAT IS GUIDED READING?

Guided reading is an instructional approach that involves a teacher working with a small group of students who demonstrate similar reading behaviors and can all read similar levels of texts. The text is easy enough for students to read with your skillful support. The text offers challenges and opportunities for problem solving, but is easy enough for students to read with some fluency. You choose selections that help students expand their strategies.

What is the purpose of guided reading?

You select books that students can read with about 90–94 percent accuracy. Students can understand and enjoy the story because it's accessible to them through their own strategies, supported by your introduction. They focus on meaning but use problem-solving strategies to figure out words they don't know, deal with difficult sentence structure, and understand concepts or ideas they have never before encountered in print.

Why is guided reading important?

Guided reading gives students the chance to apply the strategies they already know to new text. You provide support, but the ultimate goal is independent reading.

When are children ready for guided reading?

Developing readers have already gained important understandings about how print works. These students know how to monitor their own reading. They have the ability to check on themselves or search for possibilities and alternatives if they encounter a problem when reading. For these readers, the guided reading experience is a powerful way to support the development of reading strategies.

The ultimate goal of guided reading is reading a variety of texts with ease and deep understanding. Silent reading means rapid processing of texts with most attention on meaning, which is achieved as readers move past beginning levels through H, I, and J. At all levels, students read orally with fluency and phrasing.

Matching Books to Readers

The teacher selects a text for a small group of students who are similar in their reading behaviors at a particular point in time. In general, the text is about right for students in the group. It is not too easy, yet not too hard, and offers a variety of challenges to help readers become flexible problem solvers. You should choose Guided Reading Program books for students that:

- Match their knowledge base
- Help them take the next step in learning to read
- Are interesting to them
- Offer just enough challenge to support problem solving while still supporting fluency and meaning

Supporting Students' Reading

In working with students in guided reading, you constantly balance the difficulty of the text with support for students reading the text. You introduce the story to the group, support individuals through brief interactions while they read, and guide them to talk together afterward about the words and ideas in the text. In this way, you refine text selection and help individual readers move forward in developing a reading process.

Good readers employ a wide range of word-solving strategies, including analysis of sound-letter relationships and word parts. They must figure out words that are embedded in different kinds of texts. Reading a variety of books enables them to go beyond reading individual words to interpreting language and its subtle meanings.

For more specific teaching suggestions, see individual cards for each book title.

Procedure for Guided Reading	
	• The teacher works with a small group of students with similar needs.
	• The teacher provides introductions to the text that support students' later attempts at problem solving.
	• Each student reads the whole text or a unified part of the text.
	• Readers figure out new words while reading for meaning.
	• The teacher prompts, encourages, and confirms students' attempts at problem solving.
	• The teacher and student engage in meaningful conversations about what they are reading.
	• The teacher and student revisit the text to demonstrate and use a range of comprehension strategies.

ORGANIZING YOUR CLASSROOM FOR **GUIDED READING**

adapted from *Guided Reading: Making It Work* (Schulman & Payne, 2000)

Good management begins with a thoughtful room arrangement and careful selection of materials; the way you organize furniture and supplies will support the learning that takes place within your classroom. For guided reading to be effective, the rest of the class must be engaged in other literacy activities that do not require direct teacher involvement. For most classes, this means literacy centers that accommodate small groups of students. So, a strategically arranged classroom for guided reading would have a class library, inviting spots for individual work, spaces for whole-class gatherings and small-group meetings, and several literacy centers.

Arranging the room and organizing materials for effective reading and writing workshops takes thought and planning. So before the school year even begins, consider the activities you're planning for your class and the physical layout of your room. With a little ingenuity, you can provide an environment that will support learning all year long.

Scheduling for Guided Reading

To determine the time you'll need for guided reading, consider the number of students in your class and the range of reading abilities they possess. Then create your initial groupings; the ideal group size is four to six, though guided reading groups might range from two to six. Place below-grade or struggling readers in smaller groups. Keep in mind that sessions are short—often 10–15 minutes for emergent readers, and 15–30 minutes for more advanced readers. You will want to meet with at-risk groups every day; five meetings over a two-week period for more advanced groups are typical. You'll also want to allow yourself some time for assessment—taking a running record, jotting anecdotal notes, or conducting oral interviews, for example. Finally, allow a few minutes between groups to check in with the rest of the class.

THE SCHOLASTIC
GUIDED READING CLASSROOM

Scholastic Guided Reading Programs support a comprehensive reading program by integrating guided instruction, assessment, and independent practice into your classroom. Here's what the Guided Reading classroom looks like:

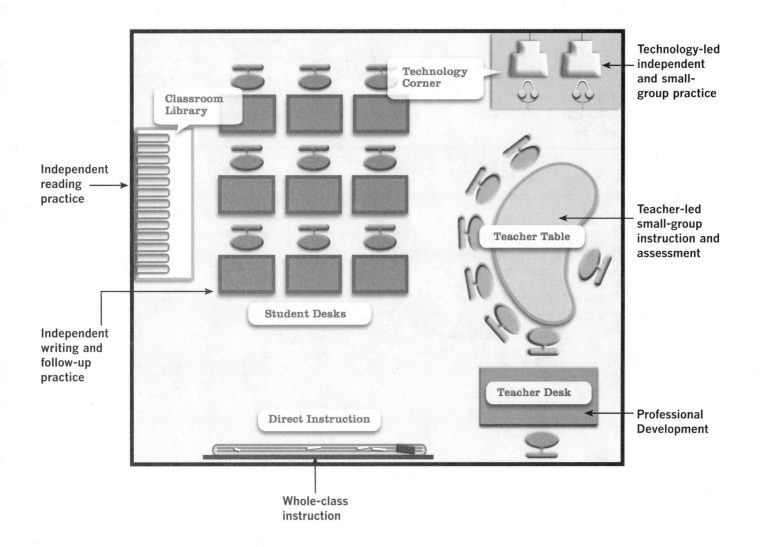

SETTING UP
LITERACY CENTERS

adapted from *Guided Reading: Making It Work* (Schulman & Payne, 2000)

As a way of managing the time to meet with small groups of students, teachers often use literacy centers. At literacy centers, students continue to participate in purposeful and authentic literacy activities. These centers provide many opportunities to practice the skills real readers and writers use. They take the place of traditional worksheets.

Literacy centers can be designed to address a wide range of skill levels, learning styles, and interests. Students work in heterogeneous groups that change often. The number of students at each center depends upon the type of center and the space for it. For example, in one first-grade classroom, the listening center has stations for four students, the computer center accommodates one student per computer, and the library center holds up to three students.

When arranging your centers, consider the number of students you want to accommodate at once, the space you have available, and the topics that you want to cover. Also think about transitions between centers—will students work at the same center during the whole guided reading period? If so, do they know what to do if they finish early? If not, do they know how to move to another center or activity without disturbing you or other class members? Establishing clear expectations and routines will help centers run smoothly, so you can focus on guided reading groups.

When first setting up students' use of literacy centers, take time each day to discuss with students what happened at centers that day. Some questions to consider are, "What went well? What might we change to make it work better?" This helps students think about ways to problem solve when they meet difficulties working independently.

Things to Consider When Setting Up Literacy Centers

- Establish a manageable number of centers that can be changed easily and routinely.
- Plan time to introduce and demonstrate how each center operates. Some teachers do this during scheduled shared reading/writing time.
- Consider the physical arrangement of the centers to permit movement and a balance of quiet and noisy areas.
- Design centers to meet the range of all learners, addressing a variety of interests and learning styles.
- Have supplies accessible and labeled for independent student use.
- Create signs or charts that communicate functional information and directions, such as "How to Use the CD Player."
- Develop a plan for the rotation of students through centers and a way to keep track of centers.
- Provide an opportunity for students to select centers.
- Develop a signal or a problem-solving technique for students to use while they are at centers and you are working with other students.
- Periodically review what's working and not working at centers.

Managing and Organizing Literacy Centers

There are a variety of ways to organize and manage centers. Some teachers have students select literacy centers, while others choose the centers for the students to ensure they regularly rotate through them. No matter which approach you take, it is important to have a record-keeping system in place to monitor student participation in various centers.

Alternatives to Centers

Instead of centers, some teachers prefer to involve students in productive reading and writing work at their tables or desks. For Kindergarten and Grade 1, remember that children will need a chance to stretch and move periodically.

For students in Grades 3 and above, you may wish to phase out most work at centers. For independent work, students can:

- Read silently a book of their choice at their independent level
- Write or draw in response to reading
- Engage in longer projects that involve research, reading, and writing

GROUPING STUDENTS

Your job is to take each student from his or her present level to a more advanced one. Therefore, there must be assessment of individual students. With class sizes ranging from 20 to 35, grouping for instruction makes sense. As teachers, we want to make learning manageable, while avoiding any negative aspects of grouping.

Fundamentals of Grouping

Assessment of Students' Knowledge Base

Students' knowledge base is the key element in selecting texts and planning instruction for groups so that they can read with 90 percent accuracy and use the skills that assure understanding. Other aspects to consider when selecting the best level for a group include:

- **How well developing readers can control a strategy, such as analyzing a new word**
- **The kinds of language students find understandable and which they find challenging**
- **What concepts they know or what concepts they don't understand**
- **The kinds of texts and genres they have experienced. For example, if they have handled only narrative texts, then informational texts may be difficult**

See pages 94–119 for help in assessing which level is best for a group.

Dynamic Grouping

Because students' individual needs change so often, ongoing observation of behavior and assessment of their knowledge and experience are essential to the guided reading process. Students progress at different rates, so regrouping is also ongoing. By grouping in different ways for different purposes, you can avoid labeling students with group names that are symbols of a static achievement level.

As you informally assess students' reading on a daily basis, you may wish to use the descriptions of **Behaviors to Notice and Support** on pages 94–119 for the level of book you are using. A quick, informal observation of students' reading will help you determine if the book was at the appropriate level.

- **Was this book too hard for this student? If the student can't read it independently with 90–94 percent accuracy and isn't using strategies as he or she reads, then the book is too hard.**
- **If the student reads with such fluency that there is no need for problem-solving behaviors, then the student should be reading a higher-level text for guided reading. Of course, the lower-level text will be useful for fluency practice.**

RUNNING
GUIDED READING GROUPS

Step 1 **Select a Book**

With students' needs in mind, select a book for a group of two to six. Use the **Characteristics of Text** to determine general level appropriateness and the description of **Behaviors to Notice and Support** to determine if students' reading ability matches that level. (See pages 94–119.)

Depending on available time, each group of readers at Levels A–J might read fewer books but must sustain attention and memory over several days or a week of reading. For readers in Grades 3–6, the goal of independent and guided reading instruction is to enable students to read one chapter book a week or several shorter selections. No two groups will read exactly the same sequence of books, and groups will change as the assessment system helps track progress.

Step 2 **Introduce the Book**

Introducing the story is probably the most important and most difficult part of guided reading, and it is your opportunity to provide most of the support to the reader. A brief introduction helps a group to read successfully with minimal teacher support. You may tailor the introduction based on the group and the particular text. Depending on the level of difficulty and students' reading abilities, the introduction includes any combination of these elements:

- **A short conversation about the main idea of the text**
- **A briefing on the author's purpose for writing and some important features of the plot or informational text**
- **A description of the main characters, facts, or ideas in the book**
- **A presentation of any unusual or unique language, such as a repetitive refrain or content words**
- **A discussion of the concepts needed for an understanding of the text by activating prior knowledge**
- **Drawing attention to any aspects of print that you consider important such as captions, headings, charts, and/or tables**
- **Instructions on how much to read and what to do when finished**

Without actually reading the text to students, frame it in a meaningful way. Using oral language in a way that familiarizes students with some words they will meet in print helps prepare them to read. It isn't necessary to introduce every page, preteach words, or give a purpose for reading. The idea is to help students to be able to move through the text on their own. Any brief intervention should not interfere with the momentum of independent reading.

Step 3 Read the Book

Once the book has been introduced, students are ready to read. Unlike round-robin reading, in which each student reads a page or sentence, each student using guided reading reads the entire text.

- **Each student reads independently and problem solves on his or her own.**
- **Reading may be oral or silent, depending on level and skill.**
- **Students may be asked to "whisper read."**

As students read, you are nearby to observe them, providing support when necessary. As they read, note reading behaviors and offer praise when students use a strategy successfully. Students reading in Levels A–J will be reading in a soft whisper. More advanced students will be reading silently. You can sample their oral reading by asking them to lift their voices to an audible level for a page or two. All students continue reading silently at their own rates as you sample oral reading from several of them.

If students have been placed in the appropriate level, they will problem solve independently. However, if the whole group seems stuck, you may want to stop the group to assist in problem solving. You might also make teaching points, such as pointing out inflectional endings or consonant digraphs. Detours should be brief, not interrupting the momentum of students' reading.

Try to choose one student in the group daily to observe and interact with, helping him or her develop reading strategies, and encouraging the independent use of those strategies.

Step 4   Respond to the Book and Learn About Reading

After students read, first invite them to discuss the meaning of the text. Then select one or two teaching points to bring to their attention. What you select to teach depends on students' needs. You might focus on the meaning of a portion of text, on character interpretation, on information or facts, or on some aspect of word solving, such as multisyllabic words. For example, you might:

- **Promote fluency and phrasing by asking students to read aloud a favorite part of the story**
- **Help students focus on key ideas and language by having them find a turning point in the story, an informational part, or a description**
- **Help students figure out new, longer words by having them focus on word parts or known words**
- **Engage students in actively exploring how words work—building words, changing words, and noticing their features**
- **Help students interpret information provided in nonfiction features such as maps, charts, graphs, etc.**

By following up the reading of a text in this way, you are helping students develop strategies that they can apply to the reading of other books. You are helping them learn the "how to" of reading and to move forward toward the goal of developing a reading process.

Step 5   Assess Behavior

The day after a new text is read, record the ability level of one child and note any progress. The **Behaviors to Notice and Support** (pages 94–119) can help you assess.

INCLUDING NONFICTION AND INFORMATIONAL TEXT IN PRIMARY CLASSROOMS

adapted from *Reading & Writing Informational Text in the Primary Grades*
(Duke & Bennett-Armistead, 2003)

Guided *Reading: Nonfiction Focus 2nd Edition* includes a variety of nonfiction and informational texts as part of its genre array. Within the program, the terms "informational text" and "nonfiction" are used interchangeably. We use both terms to refer to text that conveys information about the natural or social world, and typically includes particular features such as headings and technical vocabulary. The primary purpose of reading informational text is to obtain information one wants or needs to have (Nell Duke, et al., 2011).

It is important to note that within this program students will be reading informational text that includes:

- **Books about science—physical science, Earth science, life science, social science**
- **Books about social studies—history, geography, government, culture**
- **Books about math**

Formats include:

- **Picture books**
- **Biographies and autobiographies**
- **Photo essays**
- **Memoirs**

Why focus on informational and nonfiction texts in primary classrooms? There are a number of arguments for doing so. The available research is clear. Students need to encounter more informational text.

Informational Text Is Key to Success in Later Schooling

We have all heard that from around fourth grade on, "reading to learn" is a major focus in school (Chall, 1983). Students encounter more textbooks and other forms of informational text as they move through the grades. The tests they take contain increasingly more difficult informational texts. If teachers include more informational text in early schooling, they put students in a better position to handle the reading and writing demands of their later schooling.

Informational Text Is Ubiquitous in Society

Several studies have looked at the kinds of things people write *outside* of school—what students and adults read and write in their workplaces, homes, and communities. Again and again these studies have shown that adults read a great deal of nonfiction, including informational text (e.g., Venezky, 1982; Smith, 2000). In our increasingly information-based economy, this will most likely only increase. According to one study (Kamil & Lane, 1998), 96 percent of the text on the World Wide Web is expository.

Informational Text Is Preferred Reading Material for Many Students

When researchers investigate the kinds of texts students like to read, they've found that different students have different reading preferences. Some students seem to prefer informational text, some seem to prefer narrative text, and many don't seem to have preferences for any particular genre. For those students who prefer informational text—students that Ron Jobe and Mary Dayton-Sakari (2002) call "Info-Kids"—including more informational text in classrooms may improve attitudes toward reading and even serve as a catalyst for overall literacy development (Caswell & Duke, 1998).

Informational Text Builds Knowledge of the Natural and Social Worlds

By definition, informational text conveys information about the natural and social worlds (Duke, 2000). Reading and listening to informational text therefore can develop students' knowledge of that world (e.g., Anderson & Guthrie, 1999; Duke & Kays, 1998). This in turn can promote students' comprehension of subsequent texts they read (e.g., Wilson & Anderson, 1986), because it can build background knowledge.

Young Children Can Handle Informational Text

The research is clear. Young children *can* interact successfully with informational text. (See Dreher, 2000; Duke, 2003; and Duke, Bennett-Armistead, & Roberts, 2002, 2003, for reviews of research on this point.) Studies show that kindergartners can develop knowledge of information-book language and content from information-book read alouds and shared readings. Primary-grade students can comprehend informational text that they read themselves. Research also indicates that young children can write informational text.

USING THE TEACHING CARDS

Provides teachers with a quick and essential analysis of the book students will read and the highlighted standards

Invites students to think about what they will read

Defines genre and text type (format)

Helps students understand text features unique to informational text

Expands academic and domain-specific vocabulary for discussion and writing

Points out a feature of the text that contributes to its complexity

Points out scaffolded support within text

GUIDED READING PROGRAM
Nonfiction Focus
2nd Edition

Owls

Summary & Standards

Summary: From the tiny elf owl to the great gray owl, all owls share a common trait—they are excellent hunters, thanks to their special features.

CCSS.ELA-Literacy: Integrate and evaluate content presented in diverse formats, including visually and quantitatively (CCRA.R7); assess how point of view or purpose shapes the content and style of a text (CCRA.R6).

Author: Gail Gibbons
Genre: Informational Text
Text Type: Picture Book

Word Count: 250+
Themes/Ideas: identifying characteristics of owls; learning about owl habitats

Genre/Text Type

Informational Text/Picture Book Remind children that informational text has facts about a topic. This picture book includes illustrations to help inform the reader.

Informational Text Features

Labels Labels identify the names of types of owls.
Diagram A diagram with labels shows the parts of an owl.
Captions Captions give additional information.

Vocabulary

Academic Vocabulary
characteristics (p. 8): traits or identifying features
communicate (p. 20): to share information
Domain-Specific Vocabulary
habitats (p. 29): areas where animals naturally live
talons (p. 16): the sharp claws of a bird of prey

Challenging Features

Text Children may be challenged by the placement of labels and captions. Suggest that they pause after reading each label and identify what it names.

Content Children may encounter unfamiliar concepts. Point out that children can use illustrations and context to help them understand these concepts.

Supporting Features

Text The main text, located at the bottom of each page, summarizes and clarifies information in the pictures and diagrams.

Vocabulary Many challenging words are defined in context in the main text or shown in diagrams with callouts.

A First Look

Show children the front and back covers and read aloud the title and the author's name. Elicit a description of the owl. Ask: *What clues in the illustration let you know what time of day it is? What do you think you will learn from reading this book?*

Read and Analyze Informational Text
Cite Textual Evidence

○ If you have time constraints and want to concentrate on only a portion of the text, use the asterisked prompts to focus discussion.

Interpret Information
Point out that, in addition to the text, this book has pictures, labels, captions, and diagrams that relate information. Remind children that the details in the images help them learn about owls.

○ (pp. 6–7) *How does this illustration contribute to the information about different kinds of owls?*

○ (p. 8) *What information does the author add to the main text by including this diagram?*

(p. 13) *How do the pictures of a dish antenna and an owl support and deepen the information about owls' ears that is given in the text?*

(p. 18) *How do the three illustrations fit together to add information about owl pellets?*

○ (p. 26) *Why do you think the author included three illustrations on this page? What additional information do you learn about owls from these illustrations?*

Praise children for specific use of "Behaviors to Notice and Support" on page 107 of the *Guided Reading Teacher's Guide.*

LEVEL N

SCHOLASTIC

For teachers with limited time, asterisked text helps focus discussion

Focuses on one aspect of one of the CCSS Reading Anchor Standards

Prompts readers to focus on key ideas and details, craft and structure, and integration of knowledge of ideas to enhance comprehension

Addresses CCSS for foundational skills/fluency

Teaching Options

Develop Comprehension

Thinking Within the Text
Focus discussion on the main idea and details by asking questions such as the following:
- *Which details in the text help support the main idea?*
- *Which details in the illustrations support the main idea?*

Thinking Beyond the Text
Ask children to reread pages 29 and 30.
- *What questions might a reader have after reading these two pages?*
- *Does anything the author says here change your thinking about owls?*

Thinking About the Text
Remind children that authors have different purposes for writing books. Then ask:
- *Why do you think the author wrote this book about owls?*
- *How do you think the author feels about owls? What makes you think so?*
- *Why do you think the author included the additional information on page 32?*

Focus on Foundational Skills Phonics and Word-Solving Strategies

Words With Long *a*
Remind children that long-vowel sounds often have more than one spelling. Review the spellings of long *a*, which include *a, a_e, ay, ai, e, ea, ey,* and *ei*.
- Have children look at the cover of the book and find the author's name. Ask: *How do you pronounce the author's first name? What letters in her name stand for the long-a sound?*
- Ask children to look at the last line on page 8 and find two *a_e* words. Ask: *How are these words pronounced?*
- Have children look at page 11. Which word in the first line has the long-*a* sound spelled *ay?*
- On page 10, have children determine that in the words *they* and *prey*, long *a* is spelled *-ey*.
- Challenge children to find, on page 20, six different spellings for the long-*a* sound.

For more prompts and ideas for teaching problem-solving strategies, see page 28 of the *Guided Reading Teacher's Guide*.

Develop Fluency
Read aloud the text at the bottom of pages 16 and 17, modeling pronunciation and phrasing. Then have partners take turns reading the two pages to each other. Provide help when needed.

Expand Oral Language/Conversation
Talk About Owl Characteristics Point out that many characteristics apply to all owls, but that some vary. Ask: *What are some characteristics that are similar or exactly the same for all owls? Which characteristics vary from owl to owl?*

Write and Respond to Reading
Write an Opinion Ask children to write a paragraph to support the statement that owls are good hunters. Encourage children to use evidence from the text and illustrations to support their opinion statements. Prompt children to reread details about owls as hunters. **(Opinion)**

Make a Flowchart Have children make a flowchart, using words to label stages in the life of an owlet. Ask children to begin with the female owl laying eggs and end with the young owls being able to live on their own. Remind children to include the age of the owl at different points on the flowchart. Some children may want to illustrate their flowcharts. **(Informative/Explanatory)**

ELL Bridge
Encourage children to use gestures to show the meanings of words and phrases such as *swoops* (p. 3), *facial* (p. 9), *flexible* (p. 10), *funnel* (p. 13), *lifting* (p. 15), *grasping* (p. 16), *swallow* (p. 17), *cough up* (p. 18), *flutters* (p. 22), and *protect* (p. 29). If children are unfamiliar with a word, use gestures to help explain its meaning.

Connect Across Texts
Bat Loves the Night by Nicola Davies

Davies uses a poetic narrative, watercolor illustrations, and informative labels to tell about another fascinating night flyer. How do both Davies and Gibbons help readers think about their subjects in new ways?

Connect to the Internet
Share this website with children for tips about how to look for owls: http://www.nwf.org/kids/family-fun/outdoor-activities/learn-about-owls.aspx.

Addresses CCSS for speaking and listening

Addresses CCSS for writing

Easily adapts lesson to meet the needs of English language learners

Addresses CCSS for foundational skills/phonics and word recognition

Supports CCSS emphasis for using technology

Supports CCSS focus on comparing and contrasting texts

978-0-545-68168-1

THINKING WITHIN, BEYOND, AND ABOUT THE TEXT

adapted from *Teaching for Comprehending and Fluency: Thinking, Talking, and Writing About Reading, K–8* (Fountas & Pinnell, 2006)

When proficient readers process a text, they simultaneously draw on a wide range of strategic actions that are physical, emotional, cognitive, and linguistic. As students learn the skills and strategies they need to make sense of a text, this process becomes more effective and automatic. Eventually, the reading process becomes unconscious. In order to reach this point, students need to learn how proficient readers think about reading. Teachers may often interpret this as making sure students comprehend what they are reading. However, checking for comprehension by asking endless questions during reading can turn into an interrogation that interferes with the reading process. Having students learn and focus on one reading strategy at a time also can make the reading process less effective. Instead, students need guidance in how to integrate strategic actions and use them effectively with many kinds of texts. For the teacher, this means knowing what readers must be able to do and the information they need to access to process a text.

Readers access a wide range of information that is both visible and invisible. Visible information is what students see as words and art in the text. As they read, readers recognize letters, words, punctuation, format, and text structures, and they attach meaning to what they see. Proficient readers are barely aware of this processing of visual information as they focus on meaning. Invisible information—including the knowledge and experience of language, facts, and the world both past and present—is what readers know and think about as they respond to visual information. Such personal knowledge is different for each student and is shaped by family, culture, and community. As students learn about different cultures and communities, they expand their perspectives and make new connections. Many of the texts they encounter can become the basis for this expansion.

Another form of invisible information is readers' experiences with many kinds of text, including knowledge of genres, text structures, and formats. This knowledge helps readers form expectations and predictions about a new text, access meaning as they read, and respond to the text after reading.

Different kinds of texts make different demands on readers. Texts that students can read independently help them build their knowledge. Texts that students can read with teacher support challenge them to develop new strategic actions for reading. You can help students meet these demands by giving them opportunities to think about their reading within, beyond, and about text.

Thinking Within the Text

When readers think within the text, they gather basic information from the text and determine its basic meaning. To do so, readers must process the text by:

- **Decoding words and using word meaning and what they know about language**
- **Searching for information, and noting and sorting important details**
- **Determining how the text is organized**
- **Monitoring themselves for accuracy and understanding**
- **Adjusting reading speed and technique according to the type of text**
- **Sustaining fluency**

Understanding the basic meaning of a text forms the foundation for higher-thinking skills. By thinking within the text, readers can gather important information and summarize what they have read.

Thinking Beyond the Text

When readers think beyond the text, they go more deeply into its meaning beyond their literal understanding of it. They are able to:

- **Make predictions**
- **Connect their reading to their own experiences**
- **Relate the text to similar texts**
- **Integrate what they know with new information**
- **Infer ideas that are not directly stated**
- **Think about the greater meaning of the text**

Thinking beyond the text allows readers to understand character motivations, explore how setting influences the story, and follow more complex plots. They also identify and learn new information that they can incorporate into what they already know and understand.

Thinking About the Text

To think about the text, readers analyze and critique what they read. They examine a text to:

- **Note how it is constructed**
- **Note how the writer uses language**
- **Identify literary devices**
- **Determine how the writer has provided information, such as using compare and contrast, description, or cause and effect**
- **Identify characteristics of the genre**
- **Use their own knowledge to think critically about ideas**
- **Evaluate quality and authenticity**

Thinking about the text helps readers move beyond identifying likes and dislikes and helps them learn more about how texts work. It also helps them better appreciate different genres, good-quality writing, and their own writing.

Guiding Students to Think Within, Beyond, and About the Text

Thinking about the text is a complex process that is difficult to teach or demonstrate. Although there is value in directing readers to important aspects of the text, effective reading strategies should be shown as working together in an integrated process. You can talk about the text before reading, at certain points during reading, and after reading to motivate questions and ideas. You can share your own ideas and demonstrate the different kinds of thinking readers do. However, instruction must still allow readers to respond to the text in a way that expands and expresses their own thinking.

In your guided reading groups, you can help your students learn how to think within, beyond, and about the text by being mindful of:

* The important aspects of processing related to reading the texts you have selected
* What you want your students to do
* The learning opportunities presented by a particular text
* How students might respond to text features that could open opportunities for teaching

What follows are some tips about how to help students think within, beyond, and about fiction and nonfiction texts.

Nonfiction/Informational Text

To think within the text, help students to:

* Gather and remember important information by deciding what they will learn from the text and what they think is important
* Gather and remember information from the illustrations and graphics
* Use different tools, such as a table of contents, headings, captions, index, and glossary, to locate and use information

To think beyond the text, help students to:

* Identify new information and add it to their existing knowledge by thinking how their ideas might have changed after reading the text
* Make connections between the text and background knowledge, personal experience, and other texts by thinking what the text reminds them of and what they already know about the topic
* Infer cause and effect by thinking about what happened and why
* Identify the problem and the solution posed by the writer
* Notice and understand the sequence of events
* Analyze description by examining details and looking for examples in the text

To think about the text, help students to:

- Recognize if and how the writer uses cause and effect, problem and solution, description, sequence, and compare and contrast by noticing how the writer constructed the story
- Evaluate the authenticity and accuracy of the text by thinking about why the text seems accurate and how facts could be checked
- Decide how the writer made the topic interesting by looking for specific examples
- Analyze why the writer chose particular information to include in graphics

Fiction/Literature

To think within the text, help students to:

- Follow the events of the plot; show how to think about what happens first, then next
- Gather information about characters and setting by giving examples of what to look for
- Learn about the characters by noting how they are described, what they say or think, what others say about them, and how they change over the course of the story
- Identify the conflict or problem, and the solution
- Solve words by thinking about their meaning in context

To think beyond the text, help students to:

- Infer character motivations and feelings by looking for evidence in the text and by making connections between themselves and the characters
- Infer why characters change over time by looking for evidence in the story
- Connect the text to background knowledge, personal experiences, and other texts by thinking about other stories the text reminds them of, what they already know about the topic, place, or time, and how the plot or characters are similar to another text
- Predict how the problem is solved by thinking about what has happened, what will happen next, and what is known about the characters
- Understand the theme or message by thinking about what the writer is trying to say
- Relate the theme, plot, or characters to their own lives
- Infer how events are significant
- Note new ideas, identify how their thinking has changed and what they have learned

To think about the text, help students to:

- Evaluate the importance of the setting by thinking how the text would be different if set in another time or place, or how the story changed when the setting changed
- Notice how the writer made the characters realistic
- Pay attention to the plot structure by thinking about how the story is organized and how the writer shows the passing of time, and identifying any flashbacks
- Note aspects of the writer's craft by looking for language that helped them clarify something
- Evaluate the quality or authenticity of the text

PROMPTS TO SUPPORT
PROBLEM-SOLVING STRATEGIES

adapted from *Guided Reading: Good First Teaching for All Children* (Fountas & Pinnell, 1996)

Throughout a guided reading session, the teacher prompts, encourages, and confirms students' attempts at problem solving. The teacher helps students apply the in-the-head strategies they already know to new text. The teacher also helps students use a variety of strategies as they read. The key is to prompt with just the right amount of support so that eventually, each student will take over the strategizing for himself or herself.

Prompts to Support Early Readers

- Read it with your finger.
- Try _____. Would that make sense?/Would that sound right?
- Do you think it looks like _____?
- Can you find _____? (a known or new word)
- Did you have enough (or too many) words?
- Read that again and start the word.
- Did it match?
- Did you run out of words?

Prompts to Support a Reader's Self-Monitoring Strategies

- Were you right?
- Why did you stop?
- What letter would you expect to see at the beginning? At the end?
- Would _____ fit there?/make sense?
- Check it. Does it look and sound right to you?
- What did you notice? (after hesitation or stop)
- Could it be _____?
- It could be _____, but look at _____.
- You almost got that. See if you can find what is wrong.

Prompts to Support a Reader's Use of All Sources of Information

- Check the picture.
- Does that sound right?
- You said (_____). Does that make sense?
- What's wrong with this? (Repeat what the student said.)
- Try that again and think what would make sense.
- What could you try?
- What can you do to help yourself?
- Try that again and think what would sound right.
- Do you know a word like that?

Prompts to Support a Reader's Self-Correction

- Something wasn't quite right.
- I like the way you worked that out.
- You're nearly right. Try that again.

Prompts to Support Phrased, Fluent Reading

- Can you read this quickly?
- Put your words together so it sounds like talking.

GUIDED READING AND
COMMON CORE STATE STANDARDS

The Common Core State Standards, spearheaded by the Council of Chief State School Officers (CCSSO) and the National Governors Association (NGA), are a response to the call by the states to "create the next generation of K–12 standards in order to help ensure that all students are college and career ready in literacy no later than the end of high school" (p. 3). The Common Core State Standards (CCSS) build on research and international models and draw information and inspiration from numerous sources, including state departments of education, professional organizations, scholars, educators from kindergarten through college, parents, and concerned citizens. As a result, the Standards are:

- **Research and evidence based**
- **Aligned with college and work expectations**
- **Rigorous**
- **Internationally benchmarked**

Matched Goals: CCSS and Guided Reading Instruction

The Common Core State Standards call for reading across a wide range of increasingly complex texts. And, in perfect alignment with the CCSS, guided reading teachers strive to help students read and comprehend increasingly complex literary and informational texts independently and proficiently.

The research that supports guided reading informs the Common Core State Standards (CCSS) as well, just as matching texts to readers and systematically increasing text complexity, a basic tenet of the CCSS, lie at the core of guided reading. It is no surprise, then, that the description of guided reading, provided by Braunger and Lewis (2008), reflects the instructional call to action touted by the CCSS:

> Guided reading gives students the opportunity to read a wide variety of texts; to problem solve while reading for meaning; to use strategies on complete, extended text; and to attend to words in texts. Guided reading requires that a teacher's selection of text, guidance, demonstration, and explanation be made explicit to the reader (p. 78; cited in Kucer, 2008).

What It Means to Be a Literate Person in the 21st Century

The Common Core State Standards define literacy for 21st century students as the ability to *apply* what they know to new life challenges. And this seems wise, as information is exploding exponentially. Indeed, the amount of new technical information is doubling every 72 hours (Darling-Hammond, 2010). Given the astronomical number of facts the digital universe represents, helping our students learn how to use their minds, read critically, and get at the heart of what they need to address must become our instructional focus.

To this end, the Standards call for a special emphasis on informational text and, in a similar vein, the 2009 reading framework of the National Assessment of Educational Progress (NAEP) systematically increases the proportion of informational text on its assessment as students advance through the grades.

This chart represents the distribution of literary and information passages by grade in the 2011 NAEP Reading Framework across all content areas.

Grade	Literary	Informational
4	50%	50%
8	45%	55%
12	30%	70%

Developing "Literate Capacities"

The Common Core State Standards aim to create students who advance through the grades developing as fully literate. In the overview of the CCSS (2010), a student who has mastered the standards in reading, writing, speaking, listening, and language is able to "exhibit with increasing fullness and regularity" seven "capacities of the literate individual," or what might also be regarded as seven essential habits of mind. Teachers who adopt the strategic, exemplary instructional practices of guided reading find it serves as a superhighway to creating confident learners who can read critically, ask essential questions, follow a line of inquiry, articulate their own ideas, and in general, enjoy the life of the mind that robust literacy makes possible. As outlined by the Common Core State Standards (and achievable through guided reading), students develop these literate capacities.

Demonstrate independence	Students are able to comprehend and critique a wide range of text types and genres, pinpoint the key message, request clarification, and ask relevant questions. As students engage in lively, content-rich discussions, their vocabularies grow, as does their control over standard English, and their ability to build on others' ideas while articulating their own. Ultimately, students become self-directed learners, obtaining support from teachers, peers, authorities, and other resources—print, digital, and multimedia—that they need for their own learning.
Build strong content knowledge	Students engage with rich content through wide-ranging texts of quality; in the process, they learn to read purposefully, often led by their own essential questions. They hone their general knowledge while they gain content-specific information, all of which they learn to share with others through writing and speaking.
Respond to varying demands of audience	Students become text- and audience-sensitive, understanding that different texts arrive in different formats and serve different purposes (consider the audience of a recipe versus a poem or the delivery of an advertising jingle versus a persuasive essay). As students are immersed in multiple examples of text types, exploring their form and function, they soon learn to control the various texts themselves, adjusting their purpose for reading, writing, and speaking in ways that align with the task at hand.

Comprehend as well as critique	In this era of print and multimedia bombardment, teachers recognize that their ultimate aim is to help their students become critical readers, so they not only understand the message but also can question its assumptions, relevance, and validity. Learning how to be thoughtfully discerning is a key skill in 21st century learning.
Value evidence	Again, with the explosion of new information, students need to learn how to back up what they say and write with evidence. The ability to articulate what they believe and why—citing relevant evidence to make key points—and expecting the same of others is, today, a standard skill and expectation.
Use technology and digital media strategically and capably	Technology offers a universe of learning, but students need guidance in how to conduct efficient, productive online searches and then integrate what they learn into other media. And, students also need to have a sense of what technology can and cannot do—what are its limitations? And what technical tool is the best fit for each task?
Come to understand other perspectives and cultures	Reading in general and literature in particular have always offered the promise of opportunities to experience other lives, universes, and emotional fields. A kaleidoscope of culture, language, human values, opinions, and perspectives flashes into focus through reading, and helps to shape the awareness, sensitivity, and appreciation of a literate person.

How Guided Reading Helps Students Develop the "Literate Capacities" Promoted by the CCSS

Literate capacities begin with understanding. In order to crack open and comprehend a text, our students need to engage in three kinds of thinking:

- **Thinking Within the Text**
- **Thinking Beyond the Text**
- **Thinking About the Text**

These mental acts of processing happen simultaneously and, largely, unconsciously. Fountas and Pinnell explain that our goal, as teachers, is to "enable readers to assimilate, apply, and coordinate *systems of strategic actions* without being fully aware that they are doing so" (Fountas & Pinnell, 2006). (For a more complete explanation of these processing actions, see pp. 24–27 of this book.) But it is engagement with text within the context of guided reading which enables the habits of mind or literate capacities promoted by the CCSS.

To understand more completely how the strategic actions students develop through guided reading build the literate capacities the CCSS promote, let's look at the College and Career Readiness (CCR) Anchor Standards—"broad standards." These standards complement the grade-specific CCSS—and the strategic processing actions Fountas and Pinnell outline in their seminal work, *Teaching for Comprehending and Fluency: Thinking, Talking, and Writing About Reading, K–8* (2006).

CCR Anchor Standards

Key Ideas and Details	**CCSS.ELA-Literacy:** Read closely to determine what the text says explicitly and make logical inferences from it; cite specific textual evidence when writing or speaking to support conclusions drawn from the text. (CCRA.1)
	CCSS.ELA-Literacy: Determine central ideas or themes of a text and analyze their development; summarize key supporting details and ideas. (CCRA.2)
	CCSS.ELA-Literacy: Analyze how and why individuals, events, and ideas develop and take place over the course of a text. (CCRA.3)

Craft and Structure	**CCSS.ELA-Literacy:** Interpret words and phrases as they are used in a text, including determining technical, connotative, and figurative meanings, and analyze how specific word choices shape meaning or tone. (CCRA.4)

CCSS.ELA-Literacy: Analyze the structure of texts, including how specific sentences, paragraphs, and portions of the text, such as a section, chapter, scene, or stanza, relate to each other and the whole. (CCRA.5)

CCSS.ELA-Literacy: Assess how point of view or purpose shapes the content and style of a text. (CCRA.6) |
| **Integration of Knowledge and Ideas** | **CCSS.ELA-Literacy:** Integrate and evaluate content presented in diverse media and formats, including the validity of the reasoning as well as the relevance and sufficiency of the evidence. (CCRA.7)

CCSS.ELA-Literacy: Delineate and evaluate the argument and specific claims in a text, including the validity of the reasoning as well as the relevance and sufficiency of the evidence. (CCRA.8)

CCSS.ELA-Literacy: Analyze how two or more texts address similar themes or topics in order to build knowledge or to compare the approaches the authors take. (CCRA.9) |
| **Range of Reading and Level of Text Complexity** | **CCSS.ELA-Literacy:** Read and comprehend complex literary and informational texts independently and proficiently. (CCRA.R10) |

The CCSS remind us that students will be working toward meeting several Anchor Standards at once as they delve into a text and develop as readers. The instructional suggestions on each Teaching Card highlight two Anchor Standards. One is focused on during the Read and Analyze Text section. The other is entwined in the Develop Comprehension section on the back of the card that includes Thinking Within the Text, Thinking Beyond the Text, and Thinking About the Text. If you have time constraints and want to concentrate on only a portion of the text, there are asterisked prompts to use to focus discussion. (See pp. 22–23 of this book for a fuller description of the Teaching Cards.)

TEXT-DEPENDENT QUESTIONS AND CLOSE READING

The Common Core State Standards for English Language Arts represent a significant shift in the texts that students are asked to read. In response to the CCSS, for students in Grades K–6, 50 percent of the texts they are expected to read will be informational and 50 percent literature.

Text-Dependent Questions

The standards shift the focus for how teachers and students talk about texts and the questions that teachers use as prompts for discussion. Questions should prompt deeper thinking within, beyond, and about the text. Questions that address the shift in focus:

- Require careful reading in order to draw evidence from the text
- Focus on important details of the text that will help generate understanding of the subject matter
- Can be answered with reference to the text only, rather than questions that can be answered based on prior knowledge or personal experience
- Ask students to identify and discuss the unique features of the text
- Require students to return to the text for verification
- Ask readers to think about author's craft—purpose and point of view
- Call attention to specific words and phrases within the text
- Ask students to make inferences based on the text
- May require readers to analyze, interpret, or evaluate information

Close Reading of Complex Text

Close reading will be required for text that is complex and challenging. Close reading requires students to focus on and reread a part, or parts, of a text. The purpose of rereading is to help students deepen their understanding of what the text says and find evidence to support ideas.

GUIDED READING AND 21ST CENTURY LEARNING SKILLS

For our guide to 21st century learning skills, we turn first to Bernie Trilling and Charles Fadel's definitive book on the matter, *21st Century Skills: Learning for Life in Our Times* (2009). The authors address the skills in three categories (p. xxvi):

Learning and Innovation Skills

Critical thinking and problem solving

Communication and collaboration

Creativity and innovation

Digital Literacy Skills

Information literacy

Media literacy

Information and Communication Technologies (ICT) literacy

Career and Life Skills

Flexibility and adaptability

Initiative and self-direction

Social and cross-cultural interaction

Productivity and accountability

Leadership and responsibilities

The Mile Guide: Milestones for Improving Learning & Education, assembled by The Partnership for 21st Century Skills, the leading advocacy organization focused on infusing 21st century skills into education, outlines six new literacies our students will need for future success:

- Civic Literacy
- Technology Literacy
- Global Literacy
- Economic Literacy
- Health Literacy
- Environmental Literacy

Stanford University scholar Linda Darling-Hammond sums up 21st century learning this way: "The new mission of schools is to prepare students to work at jobs that do not yet exist, creating ideas and solutions for products and problems that have not been identified, using technologies that have not yet been invented" (2010, p. 2).

Guided Reading Makes It All Possible

If we consider Trilling and Fadel's lists of 21st century learning skills, *critical thinking* and *problem solving* seem to encapsulate what is needed to live successfully in our increasingly complex world, together with collaboration, communication, innovation, flexibility, and initiative. It is not surprising to learn that these key 21st century literate capacities can originate with the strategic processing skills children acquire through their rich immersion in engaging texts coupled with the exemplary instruction realized through guided reading.

The "anemic teaching" (Darling-Hammond, 2010) of the last two decades—rote memorization and low level test-driven thinking—must give way to robust learning and habits of mind. AFT secretary-treasurer Antonia Cortese and education critic Diane Ravitch capture what's needed:

> We believe in the importance of preparing students to live and succeed in a global economy. We don't think that the mastery of basic skills is sufficient for this goal. What we need is an education system that teaches deep knowledge, that values creativity and originality, and that values thinking skills.

The days of memorizing isolated facts are gone. Guided reading provides the instructional context and cognitive processing that are applicable to all text, including digital, hypertexted, and social-media generated, and makes the charge of 21st century learning possible. Further, the small-group setting and robust discussion of guided reading foster the kinds of collaboration that Trilling recommends. Inside guided reading groups, students work together to think critically, make connections, draw conclusions, and discuss, write about, and act on their new understandings. These are the skills they learn from reading a wide range of text, interacting with multiple genres, and, within the framework of guided reading, thinking within, beyond, and about the text they encounter.

These days, students are facing new challenges on an unprecedented scale. They need books and access to the critical thinking they offer. As new media literacies such as wikis, blogs, and online social networks burst onto the scene, knowing how to read critically and evaluate the worth of the "text" are essential. To that end, the provocative discussions that books in the Guided Reading Program evoke can provide invaluable training.

Students are reading, writing, and sharing what they read and write through a vast network of social media. In the 21st century, *skilled, passionate, habitual, critical readers* (Atwell, 2008), aided by caring, professionally informed teachers (Fountas & Pinnell, 2006), will read their way to academic success and, beyond school, into productive lives rich with the promise that reading makes possible.

GENRE/TEXT TYPE DESCRIPTIONS AND KEY FEATURES

The Scholastic Guided Reading Program provides a wide variety of nonfiction and fiction genres and text types.

NONFICTION/INFORMATIONAL TEXT

Informational Text

Informational text provides factual information. Content may be scientific or social, exploring the natural and physical world or people and places in the past or present. Informational text can be presented in a variety of formats including reference books, books on specific subjects or processes, magazines, CDs, or filmed documentaries.

Key Features

- Provides information on a whole class of things, places, or people
- Describes and explains
- Compares and contrasts
- Includes technical vocabulary
- Often includes headings and subheadings to divide text
- Presents information through graphics such as photographs, charts, diagrams, and maps as well as text
- May include such features as table of contents, glossary, index, labels and captions, sidebars, and bibliography

Biography/Autobiography

A biography or an autobiography is about a single historical or current person. It may cover the person's whole life or a significant period. A biography is written by an author about a person who is the subject of the book. An autobiography is written by the person who is the subject of the story. An autobiography may take the form of a memoir in which the person relates his or her experiences during a meaningful time.

Key Features

- Covers one person's life or a significant period of that person's life
- Is usually written about an important person
- May include photographs and illustrations
- May include a table of contents, an index, and/or a bibliography

FICTION/LITERATURE

Realistic Fiction

Realistic fiction tells a story that could possibly happen to real people. The characters appear to have problems and goals that real people have, and attempt to solve these problems or reach goals with plausible actions. Readers often experience realistic fiction as truthful and can identify with and see themselves in the characters.

Key Features

- Believable characters with human problems and desires
- Setting that reflects real places and time
- Character-driven events
- Reasonable outcomes that reflect real life
- Humor that may be an element

Mystery

A mystery is a special type of fiction that centers on a problem that needs to be solved. The problem can be missing or stolen objects, puzzles, criminals to be identified and caught, and strange behavior that needs to be explained. Suspense and sometimes danger and fear play an important part in the action.

Key Features

- Characters involved in solving a problem such as a puzzle or crime
- Setting may be mysterious or ordinary
- Plot carries the story as characters follow clues to solve the mystery
- Mood is suspenseful
- Familiar forms are detective stories, strange adventures, and tales of espionage and crime

Historical Fiction

Realistic fiction that takes place in an era of history is considered historical fiction. The story combines imagination and fact with characters as part of a fictional plot placed in a real historical setting. The setting is often integral to the plot as it affects how characters live and act as well as the events they are a part of.

Key Features

- Believable characters
- Setting that reflects a historical time and place
- Details of how people live and work that fit the time and place
- Real historical people that may appear as characters although what they do and say may be fictional unless historically documented

Fantasy

Fantasy includes stories that are not possible in real life. Characters or settings may be imaginary, or the events and characters' actions or abilities may not be realistic. Once readers willingly accept the fantasy, the characters may be plausible with realistic problems, and the outcome may be reasonable.

Key Features

- **Characters may be imaginary, have magical abilities, and/or include personified animals.**
- **Settings may be imaginary and change as characters travel through time or move into alternate worlds.**
- **Plot may involve a conflict between good and evil.**

Science Fiction

Science fiction is a type of fantasy that tells about events that have not happened yet or that could not happen in real life as it is known today. The imaginary elements are technology-driven instead of magical. The science established in a science fiction story may not be explained, but it must remain consistent to be believable.

Key Features

- **Stories may take place in outer space, on other worlds, or in alternate dimensions.**
- **Science and technology are used to create a world or characters that are not possible in present real life.**
- **The setting is usually important to the story as it affects characters and their actions.**

Traditional Literature

Traditional literature encompasses stories that have been passed down orally through many generations. Different versions of the same tale often appear in many cultures. Readers expect recurring themes and structures, such as three wishes, journeys or quests, tricksters, or heroes who are often young.

Key Features

- **Folktale:** an often humorous story that comes from a particular culture and is told orally until it is eventually recorded; includes stock characters that fill one function, simple conflicts and goals, fast action, repetitive events often in threes, and a definitive outcome
- **Fable:** a brief story, usually with animal characters, that teaches a moral or a lesson that is stated clearly at the end of the story
- **Fairy Tale:** a short story with magical characters and events; characters are usually all good or all bad; repetition in characters and actions; often begins with "once upon a time" and ends with "and they lived happily ever after"; has a more elaborate structure than a folktale

Adventure

An adventure tells a story that involves characters in exciting, and often risky, situations. Characters may accomplish heroic feats.

Key Features

- **Setting may be real or imaginary.**
- **Plot may involve danger.**
- **Stories may take place in other times and places.**

TEXT TYPES

Picture Book/Photo Book	A picture book has illustrations that help tell the story or photos to convey information.
Key Features	• Illustrations show characters, setting, and plot in fiction. • Photographs, or illustrations, and graphics help provide content in informational text.
Play	A play is a story that is intended to be performed. Plays are character driven, as they are told through what the characters say and do.
Key Features	• Written in dialogue form with character names identifying the speaker • Includes character actions and expressions briefly indicated, usually parenthetically • May include one or more acts with a clearly identified setting • Usually includes in the beginning a list of characters and their characteristics such as name, age, and identity or profession
Chapter Book	A chapter book may be a work of fiction that contains all story elements. A chapter book that is informational text is divided into segments to introduce different aspects of the subject.
Novel	A novel is a longer work of fiction with chapters and can more fully develop characters over time and place. It requires readers to develop reading stamina and the ability to follow plots and characters over an extended period of time and several reading sessions.
Key Features	• Chapter books/novels may include several major and minor characters that are fully developed. • Chapter books/novels may include a resolution and events after the climax or turning point. • Chapter books/informational text may include one topic or several topics.
Graphic Novel	Graphic novels may be fiction or contain informational text. They are similar to comic books, but they tell a more complete story with a beginning, middle, and end. A graphic novel often resembles a novel in length and narrative. The term *graphic* refers to the pictorial nature of the novel.
Key Features	• Story told through pictures and dialogue included in speech balloons • Narrative may be within story frames or at the top of a page • Characters developed through dialogue and illustration
Photo Essay	A photo essay is a series of photographs with a common thread.
Key Features	• May be on any topic but most often provides informational text • Photographer may be writer of text as well

CONNECTING TO THE INTERNET AND EVERYDAY LITERACY

Consider the way in which you relish a 400-page beach book, or confront the programming instructions for your new smartphone, or peruse the cable menu for your favorite nighttime show. While you may be using the same basic cognitive strategies to process the text, you make numerous unconscious adjustments based on what you are reading and for what purpose. Research on the nature of text and on reading processes explains why these adjustments are needed: "the characteristics of literary and informational text differ dramatically" (NAEP 2009 Reading Framework, p. 7). In other words, it is no longer enough to simply focus on our reading instruction; we need to pay careful attention to the nature of the text we are asking our students to read, understanding that they must adjust their reading processes to accommodate the differences among the texts they encounter in our classrooms and in the world beyond. Fountas and Pinnell (2008) explain:

> At all levels, readers may slow down to problem solve words or complex language and resume a normal pace, although at higher levels this process is mostly unobservable. Readers make adjustments as they search for information; they may reread, search graphics or illustrations, go back to specific references in the text, or use specific readers' tools. At all levels, readers also adjust expectations and ways of reading according to purpose, genre, and previous reading experiences. At early levels, readers have only beginning experiences to draw on, but at more advanced levels, they have rich resources in terms of the knowledge of genre (p. 225).

Why Everyday Print Belongs on Your Guided Reading Table

We have long known that children as young as three years of age (and younger) are noticing the print and print graphics in our environment and interacting with it. Increasingly, our lives are governed by maps, menus, memos, and mail, both so-called snail and digital. This just represents a fraction of our daily print and electronic bombardment. Given the ubiquitous nature of everyday print, and the fact it carries its own strategic processing actions, as well as the rise of time spent on the computer, the occasion is long overdue to bring everyday print to classrooms and to guided reading tables and help our students appreciate and process it as its own unique genre and text type.

Alignment With the NAEP

For nearly four decades, the National Assessment of Educational Progress (NAEP) has been measuring the academic achievement of US elementary and secondary students—helping to define and evaluate their condition and progress. It is not surprising, then, that the NAEP also offers guidance on the sorts of text our students should read as we move into the new world of the 21st century. The NAEP literary matrices target Grades 4, 8, and 12. *Guided Reading: Nonfiction Focus 2nd Edition* focuses on younger children, Grades K–6, to prepare them for reading literature to build the literacy and comprehension skills they will need throughout their schooling careers and beyond. All of the genres and text types in *Guided Reading: Nonfiction Focus 2nd Edition* align with NAEP's Literary Text matrices.

The feature *Connect to the Internet*, which you will find on the back of every teaching card, links the content of a trade book or an element of a trade book to a real-world text. For example, if your students are reading historical fiction and they come across a reference to a map in the book, *Connect to the Internet* may link them to maps. You can see the advantages: within the meaningful context of informational text or an engaging story, your students have the opportunity to explore and exercise their cognitive processing strategies with a website link that you can share with your students.

In addition, Fountas and Pinnell have developed a separate program called *Everyday Literacy* that provides students and teachers with a variety of everyday texts to engage with and explore—both in print and on CD-ROM. Grade-level, thematically linked sets provide whole-class instruction suitable for any guided reading classroom.

WRITING
ABOUT **READING**

Guided Reading Nonfiction Focus 2nd Edition gives students ample opportunity to practice and refine the high-powered cognitive strategies they need to comprehend both informational texts and literature and demonstrate their comprehension in writing.

On high-stakes tests, students are asked to respond in writing to what they read. In Grades K–5, students will be asked to write informative/explanatory pieces, opinion pieces, and narrative pieces. In Grade 6, students will be asked to do argument writing as well. Each type of writing requires an understanding of specific structures, devices, and features. Every lesson in *Guided Reading Nonfiction Focus 2nd Edition* offers writing options that support the development of the capacities students need to undertake these varied writing tasks.

Informative/Explanatory Writing

In order to write informational/explanatory texts, students must have opportunities to read such texts and understand them. Research suggests that students typically do not learn the comprehension strategies needed to fully process informational texts without the support of explicit teaching (Dymock, 2005). Informational texts offer a whole new set of elements and structural patterns; the strategic text work of Guided Reading—thinking within, beyond, and about—provides the instructional keys needed to open up informative/explanatory text and demystify its inner workings. Students will be able to apply these skills as they take on reading and writing in response to a range of texts, including books, articles from magazines and newspapers, essays, and historical documents.

Especially helpful for students preparing to write informational/explanatory texts is understanding textual structure—the ways in which ideas are interrelated in order to convey meaning to readers. Identifying these unique structures may be the first step toward comprehending and controlling informational text; understanding them will help students in Grades K–6 as they begin to write informative/explanatory pieces in response to reading. During Guided Reading work, teachers can introduce the structures that help define informational text as students encounter them in their reading.

Problem and Solution—The text presents a problem, offers solutions, and leads the reader to the most viable one.

Description—The text provides specific details about a topic, person, event, or idea.

Cause and Effect—The text links events or effects with their causes. Watch for indicators such as *because, for, since, therefore, so, consequently, due to,* and *as a result.*

Enumeration or Categorizing—The text is organized by lists or by grouping like items.

Sequencing—The text is organized in terms of time or an ordered progression. Watch for signal words such as *first, last, earlier, later, now, then, next, after, during,* and *finally.*

Compare and Contrast—the text showcases differences and similarities between two or more topics, which may include ideas, people, locations, and events. Watch for signal words, such as *like, as, still, although, yet, but, however,* and *on the other hand.*

Opinion Writing and Argument Writing

Students in Grades K–5 will be asked to "write opinion pieces in which they introduce the topic or book they are writing about, state an opinion, supply reasons that support the opinion . . ." (NGS Center/CCSSO, 2010). In Grade 6, students will be asked to expand into argument writing—to "support claims with clear reasons and relevant evidence" (NGS Center/CCSSO, 2010). Guided Reading provides encounters with rich and complex texts that stimulate thinking and conversation, and it prompts students to analyze texts and justify their reasoning. As students deconstruct such texts in order to analyze and appreciate them, they learn how to construct their own opinion and argument writing.

Our goal as teachers is to help our students understand opinion and argument writing from the inside out, so students can control its influence and use it effectively to frame and promote their own ideas. Students relish engaging with big ideas by reading, writing, thinking, and debating passionately and persuasively. Understanding an author's opinion and purpose and how these elements are developed in text will help students in Grades K–6 as they use writing to share their own opinions and later construct and defend arguments.

Narrative Writing

Narrative writing tells a story. Most students are comfortable with the familiar structure of narrative texts. In their reading, students will identify and begin to analyze the elements of narratives—characters, setting, plot, and conflict and resolution. They will discover that not every narrative need be fictional: biography, autobiography, and other real-life information may be conveyed in narrative form. Students can use their evolving understandings of narrative devices and structure to enhance their own narrative writing.

> **Characters**—the people or animals in a story
>
> **Setting**—where and when the story takes place
>
> **Plot**—the events that happen in a story, often in sequence
>
> **Conflict and Resolution**—what the story problem is and how the problem is resolved

Guided Reading, Writing, and the Life of the Mind

What makes all types of text so potent is the invitation they extend to students: adopt our language, use our structures, and try out our textual features to frame and share the content of your own minds. As Lauren Resnick wrote in her 1987 AERA Presidential Address:

> School is not only a place to prepare people for the world of work and everyday practical problems. It is also a place in which a particular kind of work is done— intellectual work that engages reflection and reasoning. At its best such work steps back from the everyday world in order to consider and evaluate it, yet is engaged with that world as the object of reflection and reasoning. If we value reason and reflection in social, political or personal life, we must maintain a place devoted to learning how to engage in this extremely important process. School, at its best, is such a place (p. 19).

THE IMPORTANCE OF TALKING ABOUT BOOKS

Discussing books should be a rich part of every student's reading life. When students are encouraged and given opportunities to talk about books with peers and their teachers, they become motivated to share what they liked best about a text—and what they found interesting or surprising. They learn how to ask questions to find out what other students thought about a text and how to recommend a favorite book. They experience having their opinions valued rather than evaluated. They also discover that talking about books is fun.

Getting students to talk about books beyond the usual "I liked it" or "I didn't like it" or short answers to questions about specific texts is often difficult. However, there are a variety of ways you can spark discussion about books in your classroom including book clubs, literature circles, and topic discussions.

Interactive Read-Aloud

Before students can effectively discuss books with others, they need to learn how to talk about books. You can help them learn by conducting interactive read-alouds in which you demonstrate how to talk about books. Begin by selecting a text you know your students will enjoy, or invite them to select a text from several you offer. After you introduce the text, read it aloud and pause occasionally to demonstrate how to talk about the book. Then invite students to join in. Students can share comments or questions or respond to a discussion prompt with the whole group, another student, or a small group. After reading, you can invite students to comment on what the text means, link it to other books, reflect on the writer's craft, and evaluate text quality.

During an interactive read-aloud, students learn how to:

- **Focus on the text**
- **Use suitable words when talking about a text**
- **Listen actively and respect others' ideas**
- **Build on others' comments**
- **Back up their opinions with evidence from the text**

Through active participation, students learn that they are expected to respond to one another's comments and that everyone should participate.

In addition, Fountas and Pinnell have developed a separate program called *Comprehension Clubs* that provides students and teachers with interactive read-alouds and books for student book clubs that bring deep reading, deep thinking, and deep discussion to the whole class.

Discussion Groups

Once students have learned how to talk about books, they can try out their skills in discussion groups. These small groups, each consisting of four to six students, operate under many different names including book clubs, literature circles, and topic discussions. They all are organized around students sharing their thinking about texts.

In discussion groups, students are in charge of their own thinking, talking, and writing. They have a chance to share what they think within, beyond, and about a text. As a result, interest in their own learning grows.

At first, you will need to be closely involved with book clubs and literature circles to set routines and select books. Choose books that are developmentally appropriate as well as interesting. Have a copy for each student in a group. Be sure that everyone in the class is a part of a discussion group. A group can consist of students who are interested in a particular author, topic, or genre. Some groups might be all girls or all boys.

Designate where and when book clubs will meet. Encourage members to come prepared by having read the selected book and spending some time thinking about it, deciding on information and ideas to share. Have students sit in a circle at a table or on the floor so they can see one another. You may want to post a list of text elements for fiction and nonfiction for the group to refer to as they discuss the book. Book club meetings will normally last about 15 minutes for younger students and up to 30 minutes for older, more experienced students.

You can participate by helping groups get their discussions started, move beyond a sticking point, or continue when they think they have run out of things to say. Note how group members work with each other, and be sure they give evidence for their opinions from the text or personal experience. Encourage them to ask questions, especially when they don't understand something. As students become more experienced in discussing books, you can move gradually into the role of observer, interacting with groups only as needed.

As you observe book discussions, pay attention to both process and content. Some groups may be proficient at the process of talking about a book but not about the content, so they end up saying little about the deeper meaning of a book. The purpose of a book club is for students to learn how to explore the meaning of a text and express their thinking about that text. Other groups may have many ideas to share, but they don't know how to organize their meeting. You may need to spend some time with these groups to remind them how to lead a discussion, let everyone have a turn, listen when others are speaking, and participate in the discussion.

GUIDED READING AND THE
STRUGGLING READER

Guided reading groups shift as students' reading abilities and interests change. As you work with your guided reading groups, you will be able to identify students who need extra help. Guided reading provides many advantages in helping these students. After assessing their reading levels and pinpointing what skills and strategies they need help with, you can move struggling readers to groups that provide support. Within these groups, struggling readers will be able to read more with greater accuracy and fluency, as they will be working with text at their level. You will also be able to work with them on word skills that other students may already know.

Select books that match your students' reading levels	Any group of struggling readers will likely vary widely in their abilities. Because of this, you will need to be careful in selecting texts that are interesting, yet not too difficult. Struggling readers are usually slow readers because they have been trying to read texts that are too challenging. Slow reading interferes with comprehension, but with appropriate texts, students will be able to increase their speed and improve their comprehension. Gradually, students should be able to take on more challenging texts as their reading abilities and confidence improve.
Involve students in reading every day	Struggling readers need to spend more time actually reading than doing activities related to reading. Plan daily guided reading time for these students to increase the amount of time they read with support.
Plan additional time to introduce and discuss texts	Extra time may be needed for introductions and discussions before and after reading to guide students in anticipating what they will read and then thinking about and understanding the text. This extra time will help students learn how to approach text as they prepare to read. It will also give them opportunities to discuss what they have learned and to hear others' ideas. Encourage students to ask questions, and teach them how to find answers in the text.
Include working with words in guided reading lessons	At the end of each guided reading lesson, spend a few minutes showing students the principles of how words work. Have them apply the principles to selected examples. To make this work more interesting, create word games.
Allow time for silent reading	As students' reading abilities improve, give them time to read silently as well as orally. Silent reading is beneficial in that it is faster than oral reading and text is easier to comprehend.

USING RESPONSE TO INTERVENTION IN THE GUIDED READING CLASSROOM

One tool educators can use to identify and help struggling readers is the Response to Intervention Framework. Response to Intervention (RTI) originated in 2002 with the Individuals with Disabilities Education Act (IDEA). Prior to 2004, children were identified with a specific learning disability through documentation of a mismatch between a child's IQ and academic achievement. In years past, this typically led to a special education placement. The new law requires states to identify children based on their responses to research-based intervention, the theory being that their response to good instruction is a more reliable process for identifying learning disabilities.

While its premise was simple, its results are revolutionary: students who struggle with reading no longer face a battery of diagnostic tests administered by a school psychologist which, in years past, typically led to a special education placement. Now classroom teachers use a series of systematic assessments of their choice (or the choice of their district) to determine students' strengths and weaknesses. With that data in hand, they immediately create a thoughtful program of systematic, sensitive support for these students and intervene with targeted small-group instruction, typically framed around three tiers that represent a "continuum of supports" (National Center on Response to Intervention, 2010, p. 4). The advantage of using RTI is that students who are at risk of having reading difficulties are identified early. Early identification can prevent some students from being placed in special education when all they need is a short period of intense intervention. Further, student progress is carefully monitored.

In practice, RTI can look very different from school to school, as it is tailored to fit specific situations and students. However, RTI programs do have common elements:

- **Instruction is based on individual students' needs.**
- **The program is preventative and proactive.**
- **All students are assessed.**
- **Assessments used must be reliable and valid.**
- **At-risk students are provided with various levels of intense intervention.**
- **Student progress is closely monitored.**
- **Professional development is a critical part of the program.**
- **Strong administrative support ensures commitment and resources.**

In the typical three-tier model, Tier 1 is intended to represent high-quality core classroom instruction for all children. Tier 2 gives children who are not showing adequate progress more support, often through small-group or one-on-one instruction and more frequent progress monitoring so that instruction can be tailored to each student's needs. Tier 3 instruction is typically an intensive, often one-on-one intervention conducted by a specialized teacher.

Matching Great Text to Readers

In any RTI classroom, once students have been assessed and their challenges understood, the next step is selecting texts that students can read. As Richard Allington noted, "Whenever we design an intervention for struggling readers, the single most critical factor that will determine the success of the effort is matching struggling readers with texts they can actually read with a high level of accuracy, fluency, and comprehension" (2009). The principles underlying guided reading remind us that readers need text that they can read across a range of genres that showcase a variety of text types. In this way, students will learn how to make critical reading adjustments to accommodate different kinds of texts.

Tier 1

Tier 1, or primary intervention, centers on core reading instruction—informed by the best available information on how to teach reading. To that end, research (Biancarosa, Bryk, & Dexter, 2009; Johnston, 2010) demonstrates that guided reading provides a setting within which the explicit teaching of strategic processing behaviors—word solving, comprehending, and reading with fluency—is ideal. Indeed, CIERA (Center for the Improvement of Early Reading Achievement) investigated the practices of accomplished classroom teachers who were helping strugglers beat the odds and achieve. What they found is noteworthy: "Time spent in small-group instruction for reading distinguished the most effective schools from the other schools in the study" (Taylor, 2000). Tier 1 intervention is accomplished through the use of high-quality reading materials and carefully selected leveled texts that meet the needs of all students. Guided reading instruction aligns perfectly with the goals and targeted support of Tier 1 intervention:

- **Introduce text to students, providing background information and pointing out such text features as structure, topics, vocabulary, plot, illustrations, and other graphics.**
- **Intervene as needed to demonstrate specific comprehension strategies as well as prompt and reinforce students' thinking.**
- **Reinforce effective problem solving of words using the meaning, language, and print.**
- **Demonstrate, reinforce, or prompt self-correcting errors that interfere with meaning making.**
- **Demonstrate, reinforce, or prompt using punctuation to aid meaning, reading with phrasing, pausing appropriately, stressing the correct words, or using expression.**
- **Guide a discussion—after students have read—that probes for deeper meaning and helps to extend their thinking.**
- **Link to writing as yet another way to extend thinking.**

The majority of readers, both on-level and vulnerable, will thrive and succeed with Tier 1 intervention. Allington notes (2009) that this potent mix of informed, strategic reading instruction in a small-group setting coupled with engaging text that students can read is the key to success for most struggling readers.

Tier 2

On the other hand, if students fail to respond successfully to Tier 1 intervention, the next step is to increase and intensify the intervention. Working within small groups—and providing explicit, scaffolded, targeted intervention that continues to demonstrate, prompt for, and reinforce problem-solving strategies—in addition to daily core instruction is key. Again, guided reading (Fountas & Pinnell, 2006) provides an ideal instructional setting for this intensive teaching; guided reading supports and encourages teachers to:

- Draw attention to the ways in which words work, for example, pointing out first letters, plurals, word endings, consonant clusters, vowel pairs, syllables, and the like

- Watch for opportunities as students read to teach, prompt, and demonstrate how to take words apart; teach word solving rapidly and efficiently

- Engage students in word work and help them attend to meaningful word parts and meanings such as affixes, base words, root words, homophones, synonyms, and antonyms

- Help students develop the automatic word recognition and comprehending strategies that enable fluent reading

- Demonstrate, prompt for, and reinforce all the strategies that accelerate proficient reading—comprehending, phonics, and fluency

Tier 3

Occasionally, despite best efforts through your Tier 1/core reading instruction and the intensified intervention of Tier 2, a few at-risk strugglers may need even more extensive intervention. Within Tier 3, intense, extensive guided reading support coupled with a wide range of texts students can read is still a best bet for moving kids into successful, proficient reading. Teachers may work one-on-one with students and engage the services of a literacy specialist or, as needed, they may consider referring at-risk students for special education testing and services.

In this way, RTI coupled with guided reading accomplishes two goals: it 1) develops a more valid way of identifying students who are struggling as readers; and 2) catches students at risk of failure through early intervention. At the same time, RTI elevates teachers' professional understanding of effective reading instruction and improves the overall approach to helping students who don't initially "get" reading. Ultimately, RTI moves us away from a model of failure to one of prevention.

Guided Reading: The Ideal Core Support for RTI

As Gay Su Pinnell and Irene Fountas outline in their comprehensive *When Readers Struggle: Teaching That Works,* when it comes to supporting striving readers, there are "three keys to success": 1) expert teaching; 2) excellent reading material expertly matched to each reader; 3) strong instruction design (2009).

Guided reading is a highly effective form of small-group instruction. Based on assessment data, teachers bring together a group of readers who are similar enough in their reading development that they can be taught together. They read independently at about the same level and can take on a new text that is just a little more challenging. Teachers support the reading in a way that enables students to read more challenging texts with effective processing— and, in this way, expand their reading powers. And it's this exemplary core instruction, continually informed by the teaching-assessing loop, that forms the heart of Response to Intervention.

ASSESSMENT
OBSERVATION

Overview

We define assessment as the collection of information about a student's learning, and evaluation as the judgment about the student's strengths and specific needs based on this information. Assessment should be continuous—based on observation and informal measures of reading performance. Evaluation should provide a guide for teaching decisions that will help the student's learning.

To assess and evaluate a student's literacy development, information needs to be collected to demonstrate the following:

- **How a student uses and responds to oral language in various settings**
- **What a student knows about reading and writing**
- **How a student uses reading and writing in various settings**
- **How a student values reading and writing**

The Guided Reading Program is structured to give information on different kinds of literacy skills for students with varied learning needs. The program supports literacy development in reading, writing, listening, and speaking. These literacy activities provide a wealth of assessment information.

Purposes of Assessment

As a student progresses from a beginning reader and writer to a fluent reader and writer, assessment may have several purposes:

- **To establish what a student initially knows about literacy**
- **To identify a student's instructional reading level**
- **To monitor a student's pattern of strengths**
- **To establish a student's facility with informational text**

Assessment needs to take place at the beginning of the school year to know what foundational skills students have and to identify potential skill needs. All school-age students know something about oral and written language and are ready to learn more. Some may have knowledge about environmental print but little experience with books or with writing. Others may be confident with books and with some writing.

Observation

One of the best ways to assess an individual student's learning is through observation. For a well-rounded view of the student, try to observe him or her throughout the day in a variety of settings, such as during small-group and whole-class instruction, during independent reading time, or in the classroom library. What exactly can you observe?

Suggestions include:

- **Oral language ability**
- **Attitudes**
- **Choices during "free time"**
- **Specific behaviors related to print**
- **Interests**
- **Book-handling behaviors**
- **Peer relationships**

Ask yourself questions such as the following when observing a student's behaviors related to print:

- **When the student reads or works with print, does he or she approach the task confidently?**
- **Does the student have a strategy for attempting unfamiliar words in reading and writing?**
- **Does the student read and write for different purposes?**
- **Can the student retell what he or she reads in a logical order?**
- **Does the student select reading materials suited to his or her personal interests?**
- **Does the student select reading materials suited to his or her level of reading development?**

Answers to these kinds of questions will help you make instructional decisions and set goals for an individual student, and will help the student progress in learning.

Make your observations systematic rather than random. Decide whom to focus on. Select one student or several at a time to closely watch. Keep a record for each student, noting what you see by recording it on self-adhesive stickies or peel-off labels that can be attached to the student's personal folder. Alternatively, keep a class list for easy referral.

When behaviors are observed, a check (✓) may be used. You may also wish to make a slash (/) the first time the behavior is observed and convert the slash to an X when you feel the behavior is performed with frequency. Indicating dates is helpful.

Decide when to observe. Observe during a time students are normally using books, when they first come into the room in the morning, or during a time they are involved in various learning centers. You may need to initiate the experience with students who do not independently go to books. Collect pertinent data, including written work samples and recordings of oral reading, and keep anecdotal records. Speak with parents for additional input.

ASSESSMENT
RUNNING RECORDS

An effective reader uses the visual information, based on knowledge of language and the content, to predict what comes next in the text, to check this prediction by taking in new visual information or by thinking about whether the prediction makes sense, and to confirm or reject this prediction in the light of this new information. If the prediction is rejected, the reader self-corrects.

When a student reads aloud, you can record what is read and look more closely at what the student is thinking and doing. Oral reading miscues reveal a student's reading strategies. Any miscues can be analyzed to make teaching decisions about the suitability of the level of the guided reading books being read and about the type of help a student may need. One way of doing this is to take a running record of oral reading.

Using a Running Record

Follow this assessment procedure to periodically monitor reading strategies.

First Step	Select something that is known to the student for him or her to read orally. (If it is too familiar, the reading may not reveal much information about the child's thinking.) This may be: • **A guided reading book** • **A poem** • **A dictated piece of the student's writing** • **Some of the student's published personal writing**
Second Step	Ask the student to read the selected piece aloud. Record the student's reading in one of these ways: • **Record the correct reading and miscues on a blank piece of paper as the student reads, keeping the same linear arrangement of the text.** OR • **Make a copy of the text and mark the miscues on it as the student reads.**
Third Step	Tabulate the miscues. Use symbols to indicate what the student is doing. Some usual conventions follow.

Accurate reading	✓✓✓	(checks follow test pattern)
Substitution	wet (*child*)	
	Went (*text*)	
Attempt	w-we-wet	
	went	
Self-correction	wet	
	Went SC	
Omission	-	(or circle word)
	went	
Insertion	is	(or use carat)
	went	
Teacher told	-	(or underline word)
	Went T	
Repetition (of word or sentence)	R2 (numeral indicates number of repeats)	(or wavy underlines)

Evaluation: Analysis of the Running Record

Miscues in oral reading performance help you to identify the strategies a student uses. Ask yourself why the student makes each error. To determine what cues the student depends on, consider the following:

- Does the student use visual cues from letters and words, such as *they* for *them*?

- Does the student use context clues to construct meaning? Inaccurate reading that makes sense indicates the student is probably using prior knowledge or familiar oral language.

- Does the student use knowledge of the grammatical structure of language? Again, the student's own oral language may influence a response.

Make your best guess as to what cues the student uses, recording by the miscues *v* for visual cues, *m* for meaning, and *s* for structure. One or more types of cues might be used for any miscue. By analyzing each miscue in this way you can get an indication of the strategies the student is using, as well as those not being used or those being overused. Also notice instances of self-correction. Self-correction is an important skill in good reading.

Finally, make any notes on the running record about behaviors during the session. All of this information will assist you in assessing the student.

Running Records as a Regular Monitoring Tool

For each student who is able to read some type of continuous text, it is useful to take a running record about every six weeks. Repeat more often for students for whom you have concerns. For fluent readers it would only be necessary at the beginning, middle, and end of the school year.

Establish a system. For example, you might choose one student per school day, keeping the dated record and analysis in each student's portfolio to monitor the progress during the year. Select a time when you can hear the student read without interruptions, such as when other students are engaged in individual quiet reading.

Sample Running Record

Name: _____ Date: _____

Title: _____

PAGE	TEXT INFORMATION USED	RUNNING RECORD	
4	The animals had a picnic	✓ ✓ have ✓ ✓	v, m
	To celebrate the fair.	✓ ✓ ✓ ✓	
	They all brought something tasty	✓ ✓ bought ✓ t/testy/SC	v, m, s
	For everyone to share.	✓ ✓ ✓ ✓	
7	The lambs brought yams.	✓ ✓ bought ✓	v, m, s
	The bees brought peas.	✓ ✓ bought ✓	v, m, s
	The poodles brought noodles	✓ ✓ bought ✓	v, m, s
	All sprinkled with cheese.	✓ sprin/sprinkle/SC ✓	
8	The cheetahs brought pitas.	✓ ✓ bought pasta/T	v, m, s
	The mice brought rice.	✓ ✓ bought ✓	v, m, s
	The moose brought juice	✓ ✓ bought ✓	v, m, s
	And a bucket of ice.	✓ ✓ ✓ ✓ ✓	
11	The pigs brought figs.	✓ ✓ bought ✓	v, m, s
	The bears brought pears.	✓ ✓ bought ✓	v, m, s
	The apes brought grapes	✓ ✓ bought ✓	v, m, s
	And some picnic chairs.	✓ ✓ ✓ ✓	
12	The raccoons brought spoons.	✓ ✓ ✓ ✓	
	The moles brought bowls.	✓ ✓ ✓ ✓	
	The storks brought forks	✓ ✓ ✓ fo/fork/SC	
	And some cinnamon rolls.	✓ ✓ c/cam/camon/T	v
15	The snakes brought cakes.	✓ snake bought ✓	v, m, s
	And I brought the tea.	✓ ✓ ✓ ✓ ✓	
	It was a wild picnic—	✓ ✓ ✓ ✓ ✓	
	Just the animals and me!	✓ ✓ ✓ ✓ ✓	

v=visual, m=meaning, s=structure

Calculations

Note: In the example the student repeatedly misread the word *brought* as *bought*. There are two approaches to counting this error: as one error that is repeated or as multiple errors (which the student failed to self-correct).

- **Calculation of Accuracy Rate**

    The calculation of the accuracy rate is expressed by the following generic formula:

    $100-(E/T \times 100)=AR$

    If *bought* is counted as only one error, accuracy rate is calculated as follows:

    $100-(5/102 \times 100)=95\%$

    If *bought* is counted as an error each time it is misread, the accuracy rate is calculated as follows:

    $100-(15/102 \times 100)=85\%$

- **Calculation of Self-Correction Rate**

    If *bought* is counted as only one error, self-correction rate is $(5+3)/3=2.6$

    If *bought* is counted as an error each time it is misread, self-correction rate is $(15+3)/3=6$

    The calculation of the self-correction rate can be expressed by the following formula:

    $(E+SC)/SC=SCR$

T=total number of words	E=number of errors
AR=accuracy rate	SC=number of self-corrections
SCR=self-correction rate	

Teacher's Notes

Adib told the story (pointing to picture) and answered questions. Adib is using all strategies when reading and seems to have cross-checked one cue against another to self-correct. I could draw his attention to the difference between brought *and* bought. *This book is at a suitable level of difficulty for instruction.*

Note that space has also been provided for you to ask your own comprehension questions and record children's responses.

Evaluation of Suitability of Books

If a student is reading at an appropriate instructional level, approximately 94 percent of the text should be read accurately. An attempt at a word that is eventually correct is not an error; record this as a self-correction and tally it as accurately read. By calculating the percentage of accurately read words and analyzing the types of errors, you'll be able to determine whether the student is reading books at the appropriate instructional level, and you'll be able to choose the right guided reading books for individuals and groups.

Students may select a guided reading book to have it read to them or to read with a partner. In these instances the book may be easier or harder than the instructional level.

RUNNING RECORD
BENCHMARK BOOK LEVEL A

Running Record Sheet
Skippy Likes the Seasons

Name _____   Date _____

21 Words   Level A   Accuracy Rate _____

PAGE	TEXT	RUNNING RECORD ANALYSIS
Page 2	Skippy likes grass.	
Page 3	Skippy likes flowers.	
Page 4	Skippy likes sand.	
Page 5	Skippy likes water.	
Page 6	Skippy likes leaves.	
Page 7	Skippy likes mud.	
Page 8	Skippy likes snow.	

Comprehension:

1) _____

_____

_____

_____

_____

2) _____

_____

_____

_____

_____

RUNNING RECORD
BENCHMARK BOOK LEVEL B

Running Record Sheet
Houses

Name _____   Date _____

39 Words   Level B   Accuracy Rate _____

PAGE	TEXT	RUNNING RECORD ANALYSIS
Page 2	A house can be red.	
Page 3	A house can be blue.	
Page 4	A house can be orange.	
Page 5	A house can be yellow.	
Page 6	A house can be purple.	
Page 7	A house can be green.	
Page 8	A house can be blue, green, yellow, and orange!	

Comprehension:

1) _____

_____

_____

_____

_____

2) _____

_____

_____

_____

_____

RUNNING RECORD
BENCHMARK BOOK LEVEL C

Running Record Sheet
Animal Tracks

Name _____   Date _____

57 Words   Level C   Accuracy Rate _____

PAGE	TEXT	RUNNING RECORD ANALYSIS
Page 2	Look at these tracks. The seagull made these tracks in the sand.	
Page 3	Who made these tracks in the snow?	
Page 4	The deer made these tracks in the snow.	
Page 5	Who made these tracks in the sand?	
Page 6	The dog made these tracks in the sand.	
Page 7	Who made these tracks in the snow?	
Page 8	The fox made these tracks in the snow.	

Comprehension:

1) _____

_____

_____

_____

_____

2) _____

_____

_____

_____

_____

RUNNING RECORD
BENCHMARK BOOK LEVEL D

Running Record Sheet
What Kittens Need

Name _____   Date _____

49 Words   Level D   Accuracy Rate _____

PAGE	TEXT	RUNNING RECORD ANALYSIS
Page 2	What does a kitten need? A kitten needs kitten food.	
Page 3	A kitten needs water.	
Page 4	A kitten needs to be brushed.	
Page 5	A kitten needs a place to run.	
Page 6	A kitten needs to see a vet for a check up.	
Page 7	A kitten needs to play.	
Page 8	A kitten needs lots of love!	

Comprehension:

1) _____

_____

_____

_____

_____

2) _____

_____

_____

_____

_____

RUNNING RECORD
BENCHMARK BOOK LEVEL E

Running Record Sheet
In the Mountains

Name _____   Date _____

55 Words   Level E   Accuracy Rate _____

PAGE	TEXT	RUNNING RECORD ANALYSIS
Page 2	Who lives in these mountains?	
Page 3	Take a look!	
Page 4	Goats live in these mountains. They run on the rocks.	
Page 5	Elk live in these mountains. They graze on grass.	
Page 6	Moose live in these mountains. They drink from lakes.	
Page 7	Look at the bears on the grass. They nap in these mountains.	
Page 8	Who lives in these mountains? We do!	

Comprehension:

1) _____

_____

_____

_____

_____

2) _____

_____

_____

_____

_____

From *In the Mountains* by Beth Eli. Copyright © 2014 by Scholastic Inc. Published by Scholastic Inc. All rights reserved.

66   Assessment: Running Records

GUIDED READING Nonfiction Focus 2nd Edition

RUNNING RECORD
BENCHMARK BOOK LEVEL F

Running Record Sheet
Growing Pumpkins

Name _____   Date _____

62 Words   Level F   Accuracy Rate _____

PAGE	TEXT	RUNNING RECORD ANALYSIS
Page 2	A pumpkin is a plant. How does a pumpkin grow?	
Page 4	Pumpkins grow from seeds.	
Page 5	Pumpkin seeds are little.	
Page 6	A pumpkin seed grows in soil.	
Page 7	The seed grows into a seedling.	
Page 8	The seedling grows. Do you see the little, green pumpkin?	
Page 10	Pumpkin plants get bigger as they grow.	
Page 12	Pumpkin plants change as they grow.	
Page 14	Now it is time to pick ripe, orange pumpkins!	

Comprehension:

1) _____

_____

_____

_____

2) _____

_____

_____

_____

RUNNING RECORD
BENCHMARK BOOK LEVEL G

Running Record Sheet
Whales

Name _____   Date _____

60 Words   Level G   Accuracy Rate _____

PAGE	TEXT	RUNNING RECORD ANALYSIS
Page 3	Whales live under the sea.	
Page 4	Whales are huge animals.	
Page 5	The blue whale is biggest of all.	
Page 6	Some kinds of whales have teeth.	
Page 7	These whales eat fish and other sea animals.	
Page 10	Whales have flat tails for swimming.	
Page 11	Flippers help them swim, too.	
Page 12	Baby whales are born in the water.	
Page 14	Whales breathe air through blowholes.	
Page 15	Look what happens when they breathe out!	

Comprehension:

1) _____

_____

_____

_____

2) _____

_____

_____

_____

From *Whales* by Melvin and Gilda Berger. Text copyright © 2003 by Melvin and Gilda Berger. Published by Scholastic Inc. All rights reserved.

RUNNING RECORD
BENCHMARK BOOK LEVEL H

Running Record Sheet
Plants We Eat

Name _____   Date _____
103 Words   Level H   Accuracy Rate _____

PAGE	TEXT	RUNNING RECORD ANALYSIS
Page 10	First, I put some pebbles in the bottom of the pot.	
Page 11	Next, I filled the pot with soil. I made three little holes for the seeds.	
Page 12	I planted the basil seeds. I planted the oregano seeds. I planted the parsley seeds. I covered them with a little bit of soil.	
Page 13	I put the pot in a sunny spot. I watered the seeds every day.	
Page 14	Soon the seeds began to sprout. The herbs grew.	
Page 15	Then I picked some.	
Page 16	Mom made pizza. I put on the basil. I added oregano. I put on parsley. Then we ate the pizza with herbs. It tasted so good!	

Comprehension:

1) _____

_____

2) _____

_____

RUNNING RECORD
BENCHMARK BOOK LEVEL I

Running Record Sheet
Critters in Camouflage

Name _____   Date _____

128 Words   Level I   Accuracy Rate _____

PAGE	TEXT	RUNNING RECORD ANALYSIS
Page 6	Animals in trees use camouflage. Look at this snake. It is hard to see. Its green color helps it hide.	
Page 8	This leopard has spots. The spots make it hard to see in a tree. The spots help the animal hide.	
Page 10	Animals in the sea use camouflage. This fish looks like a rock in the sea. That makes the fish hard to see. Camouflage helps the fish hide.	
Page 12	A sea turtle's shell is dark on top. If you look at the top of its shell, it is dark like the sea. The turtle's dark color helps it hide.	
Page 14	Animals on the ground use camouflage. This frog is green and brown like the plants. This animal has fur that is white like the snow. Both animals are hard to see.	

Comprehension:

1) _____

_____

_____

2) _____

_____

_____

RUNNING RECORD
BENCHMARK BOOK LEVEL J

Running Record Sheet
What's in Washington, D.C.?

Name _____   Date _____
117 Words   Level J   Accuracy Rate _____

PAGE	TEXT	RUNNING RECORD ANALYSIS
Page 8	You can find the U.S. Capitol. Many of our leaders work there. They help make our laws. The round part on top of the Capitol is called a dome.	
Page 9	Leaders from all 50 states work in the Capitol. The laws they help make are rules for everyone to follow.	
Page 10	Look at the tallest building in the city! It is the Washington Monument. There are 50 flags around it. They stand for the 50 states in the United States.	
Page 11	The Washington Monument is 555 feet tall! It was built to honor George Washington, our first President.	
Page 12	You can visit a museum. There are many museums in Washington, D.C. At this one, you can see airplanes and rocket ships.	

Comprehension:

1) _____

_____

_____

2) _____

_____

_____

RUNNING RECORD
BENCHMARK BOOK LEVEL K

Running Record Sheet
Skyscrapers

Name _____   Date _____

136 Words   Level K   Accuracy Rate _____

PAGE	TEXT	RUNNING RECORD ANALYSIS
Page 4	People have always wanted to make tall buildings. Long ago, people used stone to build tall buildings.	
Page 6	People tried to build tall buildings using wood. But wood wasn't strong enough.	
Page 8	Then people started to use steel to build tall buildings. Steel worked well. Steel is very strong.	
Page 9	Steel can be made into different shapes. People use steel to make the frames that hold up buildings. Then bricks, concrete, and glass are added to finish the building.	
Page 10	How do people get to the top of a skyscraper? They can climb lots of stairs. But most people ride in an elevator!	
Page 12	This is the first skyscraper built with a steel frame. This skyscraper was only 10 stories, or 10 floors high.	
Page 13	Some people didn't think 10 stories was tall at all. So people started to build taller skyscrapers.	

Comprehension:

1) _____

_____

_____

2) _____

_____

_____

RUNNING RECORD
BENCHMARK BOOK LEVEL L

Running Record Sheet
Elephants

Name _____   Date _____

130 Words   Level L   Accuracy Rate _____

PAGE	TEXT	RUNNING RECORD ANALYSIS
Page 4	Elephants are the largest land animals in the world. There are three kinds of elephants living today. Wild elephants live on the **continents** of Africa and Asia.	
Page 7	Elephants have special noses called trunks. Long teeth called tusks stick out on both sides of the trunk. Elephants have rough skin and big, floppy ears. An elephant flaps its ears when it is hot.	
Page 11	There are two kinds of African elephants. African bush elephants live on the **savannas**. They are the biggest elephants. African forest elephants live in jungles. Asian elephants live in wet, grassy parts of southern Asia.	
Page 12	Elephants are plant eaters. They use their trunks to grab leaves off trees. They eat grass off the ground. And they eat seeds and fruits off other plants. Sometimes elephants even eat **crops**.	

Comprehension:

1) _____

_____

_____

_____

2) _____

_____

_____

_____

RUNNING RECORD
BENCHMARK BOOK LEVEL M

Running Record Sheet
Why Do Dogs Bark?

Name _____ Date _____

122 Words   Level M   Accuracy Rate _____

PAGE	TEXT	RUNNING RECORD ANALYSIS
Page 14	**Are dogs related to wolves?** Yes! A long time ago, there were no dogs. Then people taught some wolves to be helpful. Over hundreds of years, some of these wolves changed. They became the dogs we have today. Other wolves did not change. They are still wild.	
Page 16	**Why do dogs bark?** Your dog barks to protect your house and yard. When a stranger comes around, it barks to sound an alarm. It wants to tell you and your family that a stranger is nearby.	
Page 36	**What kinds of jobs can dogs do?** Your dog's job is to be your friend. But dogs can do many other jobs. Some bloodhounds help find lost people. Their keen sense of smell also helps them track criminals.	

Comprehension:

1) _____

_____

_____

_____

2) _____

_____

_____

_____

RUNNING RECORD
BENCHMARK BOOK LEVEL N

Running Record Sheet
Owls

Name _____   Date _____

122 Words   Level N   Accuracy Rate _____

PAGE	TEXT	RUNNING RECORD ANALYSIS
Page 5	Owls are raptors. Raptors are birds of prey, meaning they are hunters that eat meat. They grab their prey with claws, called talons, that are very sharp.	
Page 11	Most owls hunt at night. Day or night, they can see much better than people.	
Page 18	Owls cannot chew or grind their food. They cough up what they can't digest in pellets. The pellets usually contain fur and bones.	
Page 19	Many owls rest, or roost, during the day. Some owls nap from time to time, resting their heads on their chests. Other owls twist their heads around to rest them on their backs.	
Page 21	Owls make nesting sites in unusual places. They may nest in hollow trees, in tree stumps, on the ground, or in abandoned birds' nests.	

Comprehension:

1) _____

_____

_____

_____

2) _____

_____

_____

_____

RUNNING RECORD
BENCHMARK BOOK LEVEL O

Running Record Sheet
Rocks and Minerals

Name _____   Date _____

134 Words   Level O   Accuracy Rate _____

PAGE	TEXT	RUNNING RECORD ANALYSIS
Page 4	Walk outside and look around. You may see rocks right under your feet. Are they gray or black, tan or brown? They might be green, blue, white, pink, or even red. Or maybe they sparkle with lots of different colors!	
Page 22	Our Earth is like one giant rock factory. Old rocks are breaking into smaller and smaller pieces. New rocks are forming all the time. On Earth, some things happen over and over again in the same order. This is called a cycle.	
Page 26	Gemstones have beautiful crystal shapes and colors. They are often made into jewelry.	
Page 27	A diamond in rock can be made into a dazzling ring. A ruby in rock is cleaned and cut. Then it is a gem!	
Page 28	Look around you at the buildings and roads. Do you see rocks? They are everywhere!	

Comprehension:

1) _____

_____

_____

_____

2) _____

_____

_____

_____

RUNNING RECORD
BENCHMARK BOOK LEVEL P

Running Record Sheet
Take a Giant Leap, Neil Armstrong!

Name _____   Date _____

155 Words   Level P   Accuracy Rate _____

PAGE	TEXT	RUNNING RECORD ANALYSIS
Page 20	Mr. Armstrong's job kept the family moving. Sometimes they lived in houses; other times, they stayed in apartments. To make moving easier, the Armstrongs didn't own any furniture. They lived in places that were already furnished. Each time they moved, the Armstrongs packed their personal belongings, hopped into the car, and drove off to a new place. When Mr. Armstrong finished his work, they moved again. By the time Neil was twelve years old, his family had lived in fifteen different places! When he was six years old, Neil went to first grade. He liked school, especially math and science. Neil read a lot in the first and second grades. In first grade, Neil read ninety books all by himself. He read so many books that he was able to skip the last half of second grade and go straight into third grade.	
Page 21	By the end of the year, Neil was reading books for fifth-graders!	

Comprehension:

1) _____

_____

_____

_____

2) _____

_____

_____

_____

RUNNING RECORD
BENCHMARK BOOK LEVEL Q

Running Record Sheet
Away West

Name _____   Date _____

155 Words   Level Q   Accuracy Rate _____

PAGE	TEXT	RUNNING RECORD ANALYSIS
Page 71	The next day Everett watched Billy work for hours with the horses, even in the deep snow. Everett studied his every move. "Never use a whip on horses," said Billy. "You can beat them into obeying you. But you'll never beat them into being loyal." "Did you learn that working here?" Everett asked. "No," Billy answered. "I learned that when I was a slave." Then under his breath he added, "That's about all I learned."	
Page 72	That night, Everett lay awake on his straw bed. Shadow was restless again. He kicked and bucked in his stall. Everett sang every song he knew, until at last, the horse quieted. Then an idea began to form. His singing always calmed Shadow. Maybe Everett could ride Shadow by singing to him. *How hard could it be?* Everett whispered to himself in the darkness. *Climb on! Hold on! Sing!* Then what he had told Pap Singleton wouldn't be a lie.	

Comprehension:

1) _____

_____

_____

2) _____

_____

_____

RUNNING RECORD
BENCHMARK BOOK LEVEL R

Running Record Sheet
Everything Dolphin

Name _____   Date _____

143 Words   Level R   Accuracy Rate _____

PAGE	TEXT	RUNNING RECORD ANALYSIS
Page 8	All life originally came from the sea. Some animals crawled out of the water and slowly adapted to life on land. Dinosaurs were the major life-form on earth for millions of years. When they began to die out, the plants and animals that made up the dinosaurs' food were available for other animals to eat. Mammals helped themselves. Some of these new foods were found both in marshy land areas and along the ocean's edge. Gradually, some mammals, including dolphins' ancestors, began to explore farther out into the ocean. There they found a buffet of delicious fish. More and more, these mammals swam for their supper. After a long period of time, they adapted to full-time life in the water and became marine mammals. Around 66 million years ago, their populations started to grow. They eventually spread into oceans all over the world.	

Comprehension:

1) _____

_____

_____

_____

2) _____

_____

_____

_____

RUNNING RECORD
BENCHMARK BOOK LEVEL S

Running Record Sheet
Neo Leo: The Ageless Ideas of Leonardo da Vinci

Name _____   Date _____

163 Words   Level S   Accuracy Rate _____

PAGE	TEXT	RUNNING RECORD ANALYSIS
Page 5	Leonardo's ideas were revolutionary. But they remained buried among his 20,000 pages of notes. Most of his inventions were not built during his lifetime. The designs were either too expensive, too sophisticated, or too controversial. Sadly, most of his ideas have been lost to time. But the surviving notes prove that he was a true visionary. For example . . .	
Page 16	**Neo 1870** James Starley is credited as the father of the British bicycle industry. Many of his inventions led us closer to the type of bicycles we ride today.	
Page 17	**Leo** Did Leonardo invent the bicycle? A bicycle does appear in Leonardo's notes. While historians agree that it is not his drawing, some think that a pupil drew it after studying a bicycle prototype in Leonardo's workshop. Others say it was drawn as a prank by someone centuries later. We may never know for sure, although we do know that Leonardo had designed many parts that are used to build bicycles, such as gears and chains.	

Comprehension:

1) _____

_____

_____

2) _____

_____

_____

RUNNING RECORD
BENCHMARK BOOK LEVEL T

Running Record Sheet
The Great Serum Race

Name _____   Date _____

155 Words   Level T   Accuracy Rate _____

PAGE	TEXT	RUNNING RECORD ANALYSIS
Page 19	Once the serum warmed, Edgar took off for Manley Hot Springs with his team of seven dogs. The thirty-one-mile trip to the next relay point was brutally cold. Temperatures fell to fifty-six degrees below zero. At one point the dogs had to wade through slushy overflow, a place where the river seeped through a crack in the ice. When the team reached Manley Hot Springs, the dogs could barely lift their ice-crusted legs. Edgar's mitts were frozen stiff to the sled handle. A roadhouse worker poured a kettle of hot water over the mitts to melt the ice and free Edgar's hands. The relay continued from musher to musher, roadhouse to roadhouse, with teams pushing west through the biting cold. At each relay point, the mushers warmed the serum over wood-fired stoves. Following the winding rivers, the teams covered an average of thirty miles each, at a speed of six or seven miles per hour.	

Comprehension:

1) _____

_____

_____

2) _____

_____

_____

RUNNING RECORD
BENCHMARK BOOK LEVEL U

Running Record Sheet
Touch the Sky

Name _____   Date _____

164 Words   Level U   Accuracy Rate _____

PAGE	TEXT	RUNNING RECORD ANALYSIS
Page 21	Toward the end of seventh grade, I saved up enough to buy my first pair of Nikes. But nothing changed. The other kids still ignored me. One morning, while lacing up my new sneakers, I decided that if I couldn't fit in, I'd just do my own thing. After that I took special science classes with high school kids for two summers. I won awards in art and photography. Someday, I told myself, I'm going to do something great, something that will make the other kids wish they'd given me a chance.	
Page 40	Finally it struck me: What if I flew around the world? I would prove that a young guy from a poor neighborhood could do something spectacular all on his own. At first I only told a few people about my idea. My dad was surprised, but he supported me from the start. My mom didn't take me seriously until she saw a clip about me on the news. Then she got worried.	

Comprehension:

1) _____

_____

_____

_____

2) _____

_____

_____

_____

RUNNING RECORD
BENCHMARK BOOK LEVEL V

Running Record Sheet
Detector Dogs: Canines That Save Lives

Name _____   Date _____

166 Words   Level V   Accuracy Rate _____

PAGE	TEXT	RUNNING RECORD ANALYSIS
Page 7	Dogs also work on trains, in subways, at shipping ports, and anywhere else that bombs may be suspected. These super sniffers even patrol the Super Bowl and other big events. Although the United States is no longer at war in some of the conflict zones you will read about, the work these dogs do will always be remembered. We salute detector dogs. They risk their lives for us every day.	
Page 27	Human handlers go through a strict training course as well. They also need to prove that they have the right stuff. The handlers take classes on canine body language, obedience training, grooming, first aid, and dog psychology. Every day, the dog and its handler play together and work together, learning to be an efficient and successful team. A special bond develops between handler and dog—one based on affection and mutual respect. That bond can last a long time. Most bomb-detection dogs live and work with their handlers for about eight years. Many even retire together.	

Comprehension:

1) _____

_____

_____

2) _____

_____

_____

RUNNING RECORD
BENCHMARK BOOK LEVEL W

Running Record Sheet
Baby Mammoth Mummy: Frozen in Time!

Name _____   Date _____

192 Words   Level W   Accuracy Rate _____

PAGE	TEXT	RUNNING RECORD ANALYSIS
Page 31	Tusks start growing in a baby mammoth's mouth before it is born. These tusks are replaced by permanent tusks that keep growing until the day the animal dies. They grow a little longer every day as a new microscopic layer of dentin is added. Dentin is what makes up most of the tusk. By cutting Lyuba's tusk in half, Fisher could count the layers of dentin like the growth rings in a tree trunk. But how would he know where to start counting? Earlier studies of another baby mammoth showed that the stress of birth is recorded in the tusk as a darker layer of dentin. The same thing has been observed in some other animals, including humans. This marks the first day of life. Fisher found a similar marker in Lyuba's tusk. He counted 32 layers, confirming that Lyuba was 32 days old when she died. **CHEMICAL CLUES** Much of what we know about mammoths and their environment has come from their tusks. Hidden in the dentin layers are chemical traces of the food they ate. By studying the makeup of tooth material, scientists can determine what food sources were available.	

Comprehension:

1) _____

   _____

2) _____

   _____

RUNNING RECORD
BENCHMARK BOOK LEVEL X

Running Record Sheet
Alexander Hamilton: The Outsider

Name _____   Date _____

186 Words   Level X   Accuracy Rate _____

PAGE	TEXT	RUNNING RECORD ANALYSIS
Page 40	On July 9, General Washington and his soldiers stood at attention in the Commons below King's College to listen to the Declaration of Independence being read aloud. "When in the course of human events," it began. At the end, everyone knew that the colonies were now a free and independent country. They cheered. Soldiers picked up their muskets and on the officer's signal pointed them to the sky and fired thirteen rounds, one for each of the thirteen states. If this was now a free country, Alexander must have thought, he had helped make it so. But he also knew that the fight for freedom between the old country and the new was far from over. It was just beginning. New York's citizens had waited a long time for the British	
Page 43	to take action against them. With the appearance of British ships, Hamilton, like everyone else, was tense with anticipation. The people of New York were afraid for their city and they continued to make preparations for its defense. They built trenches and more trenches. They barricaded the east-west streets of the city. And they waited.	

Comprehension:

1) _____

_____

2) _____

_____

RUNNING RECORD
BENCHMARK BOOK LEVEL Y

Running Record Sheet
We've Got a Job: The 1963 Birmingham Children's March

Name _____   Date _____

171 Words   Level Y   Accuracy Rate _____

PAGE	TEXT	RUNNING RECORD ANALYSIS
Page 72	The leaders were assigned to visit specific classrooms. "We never entered into the classroom," high schooler Gwendolyn Sanders explained. "We would pass by the door . . . and give a cue, and the next thing you know, they were following us because the word was out that we were going to turn the school out that day. . . . We knew which door to take them out, which route to take to the destination." At Wenonoah Junior High, guys walked up and down the hallways, calling students to come out. Kids at another school listened for Shelley Stewart to use the signal "hayride." At Parker High School, the signal was "sock hop." An organizer also stood across the street from Parker, holding a sign that read, "It's Time." R.C. Johnson, the principal, had heard rumors of a mass exodus and had padlocked the gates, probably violating the fire code. But kids squeezed through or climbed over the gates or slid out of windows. Music students in the Choir Annex simply ran out the back door.	

Comprehension:

1) _____

_____

_____

2) _____

_____

_____

RUNNING RECORD
BENCHMARK BOOK LEVEL Z

Running Record Sheet
The Dark Game

Name _____   Date _____

178 Words   Level Z   Accuracy Rate _____

PAGE	TEXT	RUNNING RECORD ANALYSIS
Page 76	Without a doubt, Harriet Tubman was the most important African-American spy. Most people know Tubman as one of the	
Page 77	foremost conductors on the Underground Railroad. In addition to helping runaway slaves escape to the North, the Underground Railroad also helped escaped Union soldiers return to their units. In fact, it was Tubman's work on the Underground Railroad that led Union generals to learn of her. When the federal General Staff recruited Harriet Tubman as a spy in 1862, she in turn recruited nine African-American men for her intelligence unit. Some of them were riverboat pilots who knew every trickle and tide of the coastal waterways. The following year she formed a regiment of African-American soldiers under the command of Colonel James Montgomery of South Carolina. Union gunships manned by three hundred black soldiers from Tubman's regiment successfully navigated treacherous waters laced with explosive mines because intelligence from other African Americans had pinpointed the mines' locations. In enemy territory, Tubman's regiment led about eight hundred slaves to freedom and destroyed an enormous cache of food, war supplies, and cotton.	

Comprehension:

1) _____

_____

2) _____

_____

BENCHMARK BOOKS

Level	Benchmark Book
Level A	Skippy Likes the Seasons
Level B	Houses
Level C	Animal Tracks
Level D	What Kittens Need
Level E	In the Mountains
Level F	Growing Pumpkins
Level G	Whales
Level H	Plants We Eat
Level I	Critters in Camouflage
Level J	What's in Washington, D.C.?
Level K	Skyscrapers
Level L	Elephants
Level M	Why Do Dogs Bark?
Level N	Owls
Level O	Rocks and Minerals
Level P	Take a Giant Leap, Neil Armstrong!
Level Q	Away West
Level R	Everything Dolphin
Level S	Neo Leo: The Ageless Ideas of Leonardo da Vinci
Level T	The Great Serum Race
Level U	Touch the Sky
Level V	Detector Dogs: Canines That Save Lives
Level W	Baby Mammoth Mummy: Frozen in Time!
Level X	Alexander Hamilton: The Outsider
Level Y	We've Got a Job: The 1963 Birmingham Children's March
Level Z	The Dark Game

GUIDELINES FOR ASSESSING READING COMPREHENSION THROUGH RETELLING

Select similar texts.

When comparing a student's retelling over time, use the same type of text each time. Compare narratives with other narratives and informational texts with other informational texts. Also select similar levels unless you are purposely moving a struggling reader down a level to discover an independent reading level or moving a reader up to a more challenging level.

Prepare a guide sheet.

In preparation for retelling, preview a text to determine what kinds of ideas and information you will be listening for in the student retelling. You may want to create a guide sheet or checklist that you can refer to and use for taking notes.

For informational texts, include on your checklist:

- **Title and author name**
- **Genre**
- **Book topic**
- **Main idea of the book and of any sections or chapters**
- **Important details that support main ideas**
- **Important people included if the book is a narrative**
- **Important events listed in sequential order**
- **Text features such as photographs or illustrations, diagrams, charts, and maps**

For literature, include on your checklist:

- **Title and author name**
- **Genre**
- **Character names and a note whether they are major or minor characters**
- **Note about the setting, including any changes in setting**
- **Brief description of the problem, conflict, or goal in the story**
- **List of important events in sequential order in the beginning, middle, and end**
- **Brief description of how the problem or conflict is solved, or the goal reached**

Ask the student to retell the text.

Make sure the student has recently read the text selected for the retelling. Then ask the student to retell the story or information, starting at the beginning and telling what happened or what the author said about the topic. As the student retells, make checks or notes on your guide sheet that will help you recall what the student included and the sequence of information. If you find it difficult to make checks or notes, it may be because the student is retelling information out of sequential order, has omitted important ideas, is focusing on unimportant information, or has not comprehended the main idea or the plot. For events or information told out of sequence, you may want to number the order of ideas students express instead of just checking them off.

Listen for what the student says and does not say.	When you listen to a retelling, listen for what the student says and how the student retells fiction or informational text. What the student leaves out is as important as what he or she says as an indicator of comprehension and understanding.

In retelling informational text, listen for:

- **Statement of what the text is about**
- **Statements of main ideas**
- **Key ideas and facts**
- **Mention of text features from which the student derived information, such as a photograph or illustration, chart, diagram, or map**
- **Use of language and vocabulary from the text**
- **Understanding of the genre, such as whether the student points out that the text describes or explains a topic, tells about the life of a person or is told by that person, or narrates an important time or event in history**
- **Understanding of how the text is organized by mention of details that support main ideas, or how the author explained or described a topic, presented a problem and solution, showed causes and effects, or compared and contrasted people, things, or ideas**

In a fiction retelling, listen for:

- **Characters' names**
- **Important events in sequence**
- **Important details**
- **Use of language and vocabulary from the story**
- **Understanding of how the story is organized**
- **Understanding of the genre, such as whether a student knows a story is realistic, a fantasy, or a special type of literature such as a folktale, fable, or mystery. This is evidenced by mention of setting, understanding that characters are imaginary, connection with realistic situations and people, or a description of clues that lead to solving a mystery**

Provide prompts if needed.	When a student is retelling, let him finish without prompting for information. If the retelling is incomplete, out of order, or leaves out important information, you may want to prompt with more specific questions about parts of the text the student misunderstood or did not include. Note how many prompts are needed to complete the retelling.

| **Summarize and evaluate the retelling.** | Using your guide sheet, discuss and review the retelling with the student to help him or her understand what can be improved and how. This process also helps you develop instructional goals for future sessions.

You can also use your guide sheet to help you evaluate the retelling at a later time and determine what level the student is on and what instruction he or she needs. Keep your guide sheets for each student retelling to give you information for determining student progress and points for intervention. |
|---|---|

Evaluating Students' Retellings

Students' retellings of informational text and fiction will give you a snapshot of where students fall in their ability to process and comprehend text. The following criteria for establishing levels can aid you in placing a student at a particular level and help you plan for instruction.

INFORMATIONAL TEXT/NONFICTION

Level	Criteria for Establishing Level
3	Most-complete retellings: • Show a comprehension of the topic • Indicate an understanding of the genre in a description of the text, its purpose, and how it is organized • Present main ideas of whole text and parts of text • Provide important details that support main ideas • Include key ideas and facts • Elaborate using details enhanced by prior knowledge • Comment on or evaluate the text • Do not require prompts during retelling
2	Less complex retellings: • Show a basic comprehension of the topic • Indicate a basic understanding of the genre and text organization in a description of the book • Present concrete related facts or events in sequence • Supply missing information through appropriate inferences • Include some main ideas • Provide some important details that support main ideas • Mention some key ideas and facts, but omit others • Require one or two prompts during retelling
1	Simple descriptive retellings: • Are partial or limited • Provide the topic of the text • Include misinterpretations • Include general ideas without focusing on specific main ideas • Omit important details to support main ideas • Do not include comments on text structure • Require three or more prompts during retelling

LITERATURE/FICTION

Level	Criteria for Establishing Level
3	Most-complete retellings: • Indicate an understanding of the genre through description of and connections made to setting, characters, and plot • Present a sequence of actions and events • Provide explanations for the motivations behind characters' actions • Include character names • Elaborate using important details from the story • Comment on or evaluate the story • Do not require prompts during retelling
2	Less complex retellings: • Indicate a basic understanding of genre in brief comments of characters, setting, and plot • Present concrete events in sequence • Supply missing information through appropriate inferences • Include some explanation of the causes of events or characters' motivations • Include some important details • Require one or two prompts during retelling
1	Simple descriptive retellings: • Are partial or limited • Indicate a lack of awareness of genre through no mention of a genre's features • Have simple beginning, middle, and end • May include events out of sequence • May describe a setting • Present an initiating event and the outcome of a problem • Include misinterpretations • Refer to characters as "he" or "she" rather than by name • Require three or more prompts during retelling

READING LEVEL CORRELATIONS*

Grade Level (Basal)	Guided Reading Levels	DRA Levels	Success for All Levels	Reading Recovery Levels	Stages of Reading	Lexile® CCSS Recommendations	DRP Text
Kindergarten	A B	A 2	1–3	A–B, 2	Emergent	Beginning Reader	
Pre-Primer	C D E	3–4 6 8	4–25 25	3–4 5–6 7–8	Emergent/ Early	Beginning Reader	
Primer	F G	10 12	26–27	9–10 12	Early/ Transitional	Beginning Reader	
1st Grade	H I	14 16	38–48	14 16	Early/ Transitional	190L–530L	25–30
2nd Grade	J–K L–M	16–18 20–24	2.0	18 20	Transitional Fluency/ Extending	420L–650L	30–44
3rd Grade	N O–P	28–30 34–38	3.0	22 24	Fluency/ Extending	520L–820L	44–54
4th Grade	Q–R	40	4.0	26	Fluency/ Extending Advanced	740L–940L	46–55
5th Grade	S–V	50	—	26–28	Fluency/ Extending Advanced	830L–1010L	49–57
6th Grade	W–Y Z	60 70–80	—	30 32–34	Advanced	925L–1070L	51–60

* See the **Leveling Resource Chart** on the back of your materials folder. This chart identifies the overlapping level ranges for each grade in the Scholastic Guided Reading Program as compared to basals.

USING THE
GUIDED READING PROGRAM

Characteristics of Text

The easiest books are included in Levels A and B. We suggest that children begin using Level A books for guided reading after they have listened to many stories and participated in shared reading. They should have some familiarity with print and understand that you read print and move from left to right in doing so. Children need not know all the letters of the alphabet and their sounds before reading Level A books.

Level A includes picture books without words, some with simple labels or captions, and some with as many as five or six words, often on one line.

In general, these books have clear, easy-to-read print with generous space between words. These simple formats enable young children to focus on print and reading from left to right, while gradually increasing their control over more words. Many of the books have high-frequency words and repeating language patterns. Print is presented in a variety of ways, which helps children become flexible readers from the start. In general, the books focus on topics that are familiar to most children. Books with more complex topics usually have fewer words and will require more of an introduction and teacher-child interaction to support understanding.

Behaviors to Notice and Support

	Child's Name							
Understands familiar concepts in stories and illustrations								
Differentiates print from pictures								
Holds the book and turns pages from right to left								
Reads words from left to right								
Begins to match word by word, pointing with one finger under words								
Locates both known and new words								
Remembers and uses language patterns								
Relates the book to his or her experience								

USING THE
GUIDED READING PROGRAM

Characteristics of Text

Level B books generally have simple story lines or a single idea. The print is easy to read, with adequate space between words so that children can point to words as they read. Books at this level generally have one or two lines of print on a page, somewhat longer sentences, and a variety of punctuation.

There is direct correspondence between the text and pictures, and repeating patterns support the reader. Topics are generally familiar to most children. If more complex concepts are involved, the reading of the book will require teacher-child interaction to support understanding.

Behaviors to Notice and Support

Child's Name							
Demonstrates control of left-to-right movement and return sweep							
Begins to control word-by-word matching across two lines of text, pointing with one finger							
Notices and interprets detail in pictures							
Talks about ideas in the text							
Remembers and uses language patterns in text							
Uses knowledge of high-frequency words to check on reading							
Uses word-by-word matching to check on reading							
Notices mismatches in meaning or language							
Uses visual information, such as the first letter of the word, to read known and new words							
Pays close attention to print							
Notices features of letters and words							
Begins to self-monitor, noticing mismatches in meaning or language							
Rereads to confirm or figure out new words							

USING THE
GUIDED READING PROGRAM

Characteristics of Text

Level C books have simple story lines and topics that are familiar to most children. Some may offer a new viewpoint on a familiar topic. Level C books generally have more words and lines of print than books at earlier levels. Print is clear and readable, with adequate space between words. Most sentences are simple, but some have more complex structure, offering readers a challenge. While Level C books include some repeating language patterns, these are more complex and there is a shift to more varied patterns. Language patterns are more likely to change from page to page, so children cannot rely on them to make predictions and must pay closer attention to print. Level C books include many high-frequency words, as well as easily decodable words.

Behaviors to Notice and Support

	Child's Name							
Demonstrates control of left-to-right directionality and word-by-word matching across several lines of print								
Begins to track print with eyes								
Rereads to solve problems, such as figuring out new words								
Demonstrates awareness of punctuation by pausing and using some phrasing								
Uses picture details to help figure out words								
Remembers and uses language patterns in text								
Rereads to confirm or figure out new words								
Solves some new words independently								
Controls directionality and word-by-word matching with eyes, using finger at points of difficulty								
Uses visual information to predict, check, and confirm reading								
Recognizes known words quickly and uses them to figure out the meaning of new words								
Searches for understanding while reading								

USING THE
GUIDED READING PROGRAM

Characteristics of Text

Stories at Level D are slightly more complex than at previous levels. Generally, Level D books have topics that are familiar to most children, but also include some abstract or unfamiliar ideas. Text layout is still easy to follow, with both large and small print. Sentences are a little longer than at Level C. Some are carried over to the next page or several pages

and use a full range of punctuation. There are more compound words, multisyllabic words, and words with a variety of inflectional endings. Illustrations are still supportive, but less so than at the previous level, requiring the reader to pay more attention to print.

Behaviors to Notice and Support

	Child's Name						
Remembers language patterns and repeating events over longer stretches of text							
Self-corrects, using visual information							
Controls directionality and word-by-word matching with eyes, using finger only at points of difficulty							
Searches for understanding while reading							
Remembers details from the text and pictures							
Pays close attention to words and their structural features (for example, endings)							
Reads fluently, with phrasing							
Rereads to confirm or figure out new words							
Solves new words using knowledge of sound/letter relationships and word parts							

LEVEL E

USING THE
GUIDED READING PROGRAM

Characteristics of Text

Level E books are generally longer than books at previous levels, with either more pages or more lines of text on a page. Some have sentences that carry over several pages and have a full range of punctuation. The text structure is generally more complex: stories have more or longer episodes, and informational books have more difficult ideas and concepts. However, in texts with more difficult concepts, there are usually repeating language patterns that offer some support. There are more multisyllabic and compound words at this level.

Behaviors to Notice and Support

	Child's Name							
Tracks print with eyes except at points of difficulty								
Uses language syntax and meaning to read fluently, with phrasing								
Demonstrates awareness of punctuation by pausing, phrasing, and reading with inflection								
Rereads to self-monitor or self-correct phrasing and expression								
Recognizes many words quickly and automatically								
Figures out some longer words by taking them apart								
Relates texts to others previously read								
Reads for meaning but checks with the visual aspects of print (letters, sounds, words)								
Rereads to search for meaning and accuracy								
Remembers details and uses them to clarify meaning								
Demonstrates understanding by talking about text after reading								

USING THE
GUIDED READING PROGRAM

Characteristics of Text

In general, texts at Level F are longer and have more story episodes than at previous levels. There are also shorter texts with some unusual language patterns. Books have some concepts unfamiliar to children and some are even abstract, requiring reflection. Pictures continue to support reading, but closer attention to print is required. Language patterns are more characteristic of written language than of spoken language. Some Level F books have smaller print and more words and lines of text. There are many more new words and a greater variety of high-frequency words. A full range of punctuation is used to enhance meaning.

Behaviors to Notice and Support

	Child's Name							
Tracks print with eyes, using the finger only at points of difficulty								
Demonstrates awareness of punctuation by pausing, phrasing, and reading with inflection								
Uses syntax of written language to figure out new words and their meaning								
Uses sound/letter relationships, word parts, and other visual information to figure out new words								
Uses known words to figure out new words								
Uses multiple sources of information to search and self-correct								
Figures out longer words while reading for meaning								
Rereads to figure out words, self-correct, or improve phrasing and expression								
Rereads to search for meaning								
Recognizes most words quickly and automatically								
Moves quickly through the text								
Reads fluently, with phrasing								
Talks about ideas in the text and relates them to his or her experiences and to other texts								

USING THE
GUIDED READING PROGRAM

LEVEL G

Characteristics of Text

Most books at Level G are not repetitive. These books include a variety of patterns. Knowledge of punctuation is important in understanding what the sentence means and how it should be spoken. Vocabulary is more challenging, with a greater range of words and more difficult words, including some that are technical and require content knowledge. Concepts and ideas may be less familiar than at previous levels. Level G books have a greater variety of styles of print and text layout, requiring close attention to print and flexibility on the part of the reader.

Behaviors to Notice and Support

	Child's Name							
Reads fluently and rapidly, with appropriate phrasing								
Follows print with eyes, occasionally using finger at points of difficulty								
Notices and uses punctuation to assist smooth reading								
Recognizes most words quickly and automatically								
Uses sound/letter relationships, known words, and word parts to figure out new words								
Uses meaning, visual information, and language syntax to figure out words								
Rereads to figure out words, self-correct, or improve phrasing and expression								
Rereads to search for meaning								
Remembers details to support the accumulation of meaning throughout the text								
Uses pictures for information but does not rely on them to make predictions								

USING THE
GUIDED READING PROGRAM

Characteristics of Text

Level H books are similar in difficulty to Level G, but Level H has a wider variety, including books with poetic or literary language. Sentences vary in length and difficulty, and some complex sentences carry over several pages. Children will need to be familiar with the syntactic patterns that occur.

Books have fewer repeating events and language patterns, requiring more control of aspects of print. The vocabulary is expanded and includes words that are less frequently used in oral language. The size of print varies widely.

Behaviors to Notice and Support

	Child's Name						
Reads fluently and rapidly, with appropriate phrasing							
Follows the text with eyes, using finger only at points of particular difficulty							
Notices and uses punctuation to assist smooth reading							
Recognizes most words rapidly							
Uses sound/letter relationships, known words, and word parts to figure out new words							
Uses meaning, visual information, and language syntax to solve problems							
Rereads phrases to figure out words, self-correct, or improve phrasing and expression							
Rereads to search for meaning							
Remembers details to support meaning accumulated through the text							
Uses pictures for information but does not rely on them to make predictions							
Searches for meaning while reading, stopping to think or talk about ideas							

USING THE
GUIDED READING PROGRAM

Characteristics of Text

In general, the books at Level I are longer and more complex than at Levels G and H. The size of print is smaller and there are many more lines of print on the page. Books have longer sentences and paragraphs. There are more multisyllabic words, requiring complex word-solving skills. This level offers a greater variety of texts, including some that are informational, with technical language. Events in the text are more highly elaborated. Illustrations enhance the story, but provide low support for understanding meaning.

Behaviors to Notice and Support

	Child's Name							
Actively figures out new words, using a range of strategies								
Follows the print with eyes								
Reads fluently, slowing down to figure out new words and then resuming speed								
Begins to silently read some of the text								
In oral reading, rereads some words or phrases to self-correct or improve expression								
Rereads to search for meaning								
Flexibly uses meaning, language syntax, and visual information to figure out new words and to monitor reading								
Self-corrects errors that cause loss of meaning								
Rereads when necessary to self-correct, but not as a habit								
Demonstrates understanding of the story and characters								
Goes beyond the text in discussions and interpretations								
Sustains problem solving and development of meaning through a longer text and over a two- or three-day period								

USING THE
GUIDED READING PROGRAM

Characteristics of Text

Although it supports essentially the same reading behaviors, Level J offers books that are more difficult and varied than those at Level I. It includes informational books with new concepts and beginning chapter books with complex narratives and memorable characters. The amount of print varies; some Level J books have full pages of text with few illustrations. Generally, illustrations enhance the text but offer little support for understanding text meaning or figuring out new words. The difficulty of the language also varies. There are books with easy and familiar language and others with literary language or other challenges. Texts have many high-frequency words but may also have unfamiliar and/or technical words.

Behaviors to Notice and Support

	Child's Name							
Uses multiple sources of information to process text smoothly								
Uses multiple strategies to figure out new words while focusing on meaning								
Analyzes words from left to right, using knowledge of sound/letter relationships								
Uses known words and word parts to figure out new words								
Reads fluently, slowing down to figure out new words and then resuming speed								
Flexibly uses meaning, language syntax, and visual information to monitor reading								
Self-corrects errors that cause loss of meaning								
Rereads when necessary to self-correct, but not as a habit								
Rereads to search for meaning								
Demonstrates understanding of the story and characters								
Goes beyond the text in discussions and interpretations								
Sustains problem solving and development of meaning through a longer text read over several days								
Silently reads sections of text								
Makes inferences, predicts, and analyzes character and plot								

USING THE
GUIDED READING PROGRAM

Characteristics of Text

The Level K collection includes longer chapter books with memorable characters, shorter informational books with technical language and new concepts, and literary texts with illustrations that enhance meaning. Stories have multiple episodes related to a single plot. Some stories have to do with times, places, and characters outside children's experiences.

Readers will need to use a variety of strategies to figure out new writing styles. At this level, most reading will be silent, although teachers will always sample oral reading or invite children to read aloud for emphasis or enjoyment in group sessions. It will take more than one sitting for children to read some of the longer chapter books.

Behaviors to Notice and Support

	Child's Name							
Integrates multiple sources of information while reading with fluency								
When reading orally, reads rapidly, with phrasing, slowing down to problem solve and then resuming speed								
Reads silently much of the time								
Demonstrates understanding of the text after silent reading								
Makes inferences, predicts, and analyzes character and plot								
Flexibly uses multiple word-solving strategies while focusing on meaning								
Goes beyond the text in understanding of problems and characters								
Demonstrates facility in interpreting the text								
Sustains attention to meaning and interpretation of a longer text read over several days								

GUIDED READING Nonfiction Focus 2nd Edition

USING THE
GUIDED READING PROGRAM

Characteristics of Text

In general, reading behaviors for Level L are the same as for Level K except they are applied to longer and/or more complex books. At Level L there is greater variety of texts, including informational books, biographies, chapter books, and some longer, highly literary, or informational picture books.

Chapter books have more sophisticated plots and characters that are developed throughout the text. Some books have abstract or symbolic themes that require higher-level conceptual understandings. Texts contain an expanded vocabulary with many multisyllabic words.

Behaviors to Notice and Support

Child's Name								
Integrates multiple sources of information while reading with fluency								
When reading orally, reads rapidly, with phrasing								
Reads orally, with accuracy, not stopping to self-correct in the interest of fluency and phrasing								
In oral reading, uses multiple word-solving strategies with longer words								
Reads silently most of the time								
Demonstrates understanding and facility in interpreting the text after silent reading								
After reading longer sections of a text, predicts events, outcomes, problem resolutions, and character changes								
Makes connections between the text read and other books								
Sustains attention to meaning and interpretation of a longer text read over several days								

USING THE
GUIDED READING PROGRAM

Characteristics of Text

Level M books have a variety of formats. Topics vary widely, and include subjects that will be familiar to children as well as those that are new. Literary selections have complex language and subtle meanings that require interpretation and background knowledge.

Chapter books are longer with few pictures. This requires readers to have mastery of the text. Many books have small print and little space between words. Vocabulary is expanded, and many words require background knowledge for comprehension.

Behaviors to Notice and Support

	Child's Name							
Uses multiple sources of information to figure out words rapidly while focusing on meaning								
Flexibly applies word-solving strategies to more-complex, multisyllabic words								
Demonstrates facility in interpreting text while reading orally, with fluency and phrasing								
Reads orally with high accuracy in most instances, not stopping to self-correct errors in the interest of fluency and phrasing								
Reads silently, except during assessment or to demonstrate text interpretation								
After reading longer sections of text, predicts outcomes, problem resolutions, and character changes								
Remembers details and sustains attention to meaning through a longer text								
Demonstrates understanding and facility at interpretation after silent reading								
Makes connections between the text read and other books								
Goes beyond the text to make more sophisticated interpretations								

USING THE GUIDED READING PROGRAM

Characteristics of Text

The Level N collection includes longer texts in a variety of genres. There are chapter books that present memorable characters developed through literary devices such as humor, irony, and whimsy. There are informational books and books that offer mystery and suspense. Level N also has shorter selections that provide opportunity to interpret texts and go beyond them. Vocabulary continues to expand, and topics go well beyond children's own experiences.

Behaviors to Notice and Support

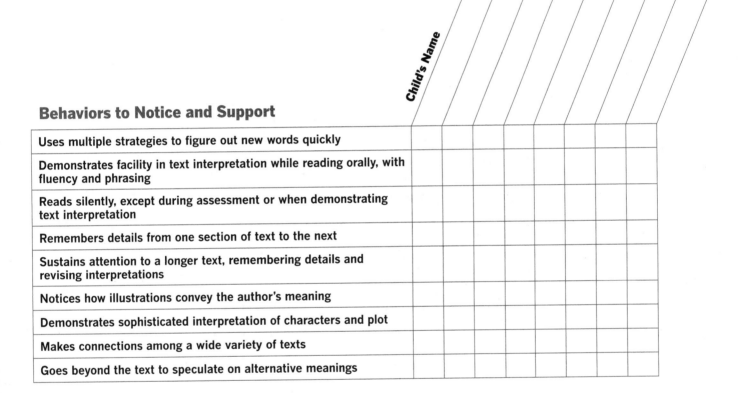

	Child's Name							
Uses multiple strategies to figure out new words quickly								
Demonstrates facility in text interpretation while reading orally, with fluency and phrasing								
Reads silently, except during assessment or when demonstrating text interpretation								
Remembers details from one section of text to the next								
Sustains attention to a longer text, remembering details and revising interpretations								
Notices how illustrations convey the author's meaning								
Demonstrates sophisticated interpretation of characters and plot								
Makes connections among a wide variety of texts								
Goes beyond the text to speculate on alternative meanings								

LEVEL O

USING THE
GUIDED READING PROGRAM

Characteristics of Text

Books at Level O include selections from children's literature and chapter books. Books at this level explore more mature themes and topics that go beyond students' experiences and expand them. Students can empathize with characters and learn about the lives of others. The vocabulary is sophisticated and varied. Most words will be known or within students' control; however, many will require interpretation of meaning. Many new multisyllabic words are included. Sentences are more complex and use a full range of punctuation.

Behaviors to Notice and Support

	Student's Name							
Solves words quickly and automatically while focusing on meaning								
Searches to understand the subtle shades of meaning that words can convey								
Demonstrates facility in text interpretation while reading orally, with fluency and phrasing								
In oral reading, figures out new words rapidly while reading smoothly and expressively								
Sustains attention to a text read over several days, remembering details and revising interpretations as new events are encountered								
After reading silently, demonstrates understanding and sophistication in text interpretation								
Makes connections among texts to enhance interpretation								
Goes beyond the text to speculate on alternative meanings								
Shows the ability to summarize the text in writing								

USING THE
GUIDED READING PROGRAM

Characteristics of Text

In general, books at this level are longer and ideas and language are more complex than at previous levels. Level P has a variety of informational texts, including history and biography. Through this variety, students become familiar with texts that are organized differently and learn how to gain information from them. Other genres include chapter books that explore the problems of early adolescence.

Behaviors to Notice and Support

	Student's Name							
When reading silently, reads rapidly and with attention to meaning								
Actively acquires new vocabulary through reading								
Demonstrates facility in text interpretation while reading orally, with fluency and phrasing								
In oral reading, figures out new words rapidly while reading smoothly and expressively								
Sustains attention to a text read over many days, remembering details and revising interpretations as new events are encountered								
Demonstrates interest in reading an extended text over a longer time period								
After reading silently, demonstrates understanding and sophistication in interpreting meaning								
Compares the text with other books in an analytic way								
Goes beyond the text to speculate on alternative meanings								
Shows the ability to summarize and extend the text in writing								

LEVEL Q

USING THE GUIDED READING PROGRAM

Characteristics of Text

Level Q includes literature selections with sophisticated humor, complex plots, and memorable characters. Themes at this level are sophisticated and require interpretation. They serve as a good foundation for group discussion. Illustrations and their relationship to the text can be examined as well. Books have complex structures and difficult words that offer challenges. There are some words from languages other than English. Longer texts require an extended time period to read.

Behaviors to Notice and Support

	Student's Name						
Reads rapidly, with attention to meaning, when reading silently							
Actively acquires new vocabulary through reading							
Demonstrates facility in text interpretation while reading orally, with fluency and phrasing							
In oral reading, figures out new words rapidly while reading smoothly and expressively							
Sustains attention to a text read over many days, remembering details and revising interpretations as new events are encountered							
Demonstrates interest in reading an extended text over a longer time period							
Uses illustrations to help analyze text meaning							
After reading silently, demonstrates understanding and sophistication in interpreting meaning							
Compares the text to other books in an analytic way							
Goes beyond the text to speculate on alternative meanings							
Goes beyond the text to interpret characters' thoughts and feelings							
Shows the ability to analyze and extend the text in writing							

USING THE
GUIDED READING PROGRAM

Characteristics of Text

At Level R, both fiction and nonfiction have a range of historical place and time settings, giving students an opportunity to empathize with characters and learn about their lives and the times and places in which they lived. In general, skills are the same as at Level Q, but are extended over a wider variety of texts. Some books require sustained reading over a longer time period. Vocabulary and language are sophisticated and offer challenges to the reader.

Behaviors to Notice and Support

	Student's Name							
Reads rapidly, both orally and silently, while focusing on meaning								
Actively acquires new vocabulary through reading								
Sustains attention to a text read over many days, remembering details and revising interpretations as new events are encountered								
Demonstrates interest in reading an extended text over a longer time period								
Extends the text in various ways, including through research								
Demonstrates interest and ability in interpreting shorter selections								
Uses illustrations to help analyze text meaning								
After reading silently, demonstrates understanding and sophistication in interpreting meaning								
Uses comparison with other texts to assist interpretation								
Goes beyond the text to interpret characters' thoughts and feelings and to speculate on alternative meanings								
Demonstrates all interpretive and analytic skills in writing								

LEVEL S

USING THE
GUIDED READING PROGRAM

Characteristics of Text

Level S includes literary selections, highly literary or informational picture books, and chapter books in a variety of genres. The collection reflects a wide variety of topics, cultures, and historical settings. Sentences and paragraphs at this level are complex.

Words present many shades of meaning which readers must interpret from the text and their own background knowledge. Selections offer opportunities for readers to make connections with other books they have read at earlier levels.

Behaviors to Notice and Support

Student's Name								
Reads rapidly, both orally and silently, with attention to meaning								
Rapidly acquires new vocabulary through reading								
Sustains attention to a text read over many days, remembering details and revising interpretations as new events are encountered								
Demonstrates interest and ability in interpreting shorter selections								
Demonstrates flexibility in reading many different kinds of texts								
After reading silently, demonstrates understanding and sophistication in interpreting meaning								
Goes beyond the text to interpret characters' thoughts and feelings and to speculate on alternative meanings								
Demonstrates all analytic and interpretive skills in writing								
Extends text meaning through research, writing, or the arts								

USING THE
GUIDED READING PROGRAM

Characteristics of Text

The Level T collection has a great variety of genres. Short selections include informational books, legends, historical fiction, and folktales. Chapter books include autobiographies, historical narratives, realistic fiction, science fiction, and other fantasy stories. Some chapter books are quite long and require reading over an extended time. Judgment is needed as to whether students can sustain interest for these longer selections. Selections contain many sophisticated, multisyllabic words, and readers will need to consider both their literal and connotative meanings.

Behaviors to Notice and Support

	Student's Name						
Reads rapidly, both orally and silently, with attention to meaning							
In oral and silent reading, figures out new words automatically and easily interprets word meaning							
Sustains attention to a text read over many days, remembering details and revising interpretations as new events are encountered							
Demonstrates interest and ability in interpreting shorter selections							
Demonstrates flexibility in reading texts of different styles and genres							
After reading silently, demonstrates understanding and ability to analyze characters and plot							
Reflects knowledge of literary genre in conversation and writing							
Extends and demonstrates understanding of the text through writing in a variety of genres							
Extends and demonstrates understanding of the text through public speaking, research, or the arts							

USING THE
GUIDED READING PROGRAM

Characteristics of Text

Text at Level U requires readers to employ a wide range of sophisticated reading strategies that approach adult levels. The difference, of course, is that elementary and middle school students are still gaining the world experience and content knowledge, or the accumulation of text experience, needed to deeply understand the more complex texts they will be reading at Levels U through Z. By this time, students have built an integrated processing system, but they need to apply their strategies to increasingly difficult levels of text. As they do so, reading with fluency and understanding, they will expand and build their reading strategies.

Fiction texts at Level U may have several different themes and multiple story lines. Texts are increasingly literary, with writers expressing layers of meaning through symbolism. Themes are more abstract; creative formats may be used, such as collections of short stories that build meaning over different texts, or novels that incorporate diaries, poetry, or stories within stories. Generally, there are more characters to follow and their development is more complex; there are plots and subplots. Informational texts at Level U cover a wide range of topics and present specific, technical information. As with earlier levels, illustrations require interpretation and connection to text.

Behaviors to Notice and Support

Student's Name						
Notices graphic illustrations and gets information from them						
Synthesizes information from graphic information with the body of the text						
Uses the table of contents to help in understanding the organization of the text						
Grasps "layers" of meaning in a story; for example, specific understandings plus the "bigger picture"						
Reads, understands, and appreciates literary language						
Interprets illustrations and their connections to the text						
Keeps up with several different themes and many characters						
Interprets characters' motives and the influences on their development						
Recognizes and appreciates a wide range of genres, both fiction and nonfiction						
Notices and uses a full range of punctuation, including more rarely used forms such as dashes						
Learns technical words from reading						
Uses reading to learn about self and others						

USING THE
GUIDED READING PROGRAM

Characteristics of Text

At Level V, readers employ essentially the same range of strategies as at the previous level, but more background knowledge will be required for true understanding. Also, students will be rapidly adding to their reading vocabularies. Fiction includes science fiction that presents sophisticated ideas and concepts. In many works of realistic or historical fiction, the writer is conveying a significant message beyond the story. Readers must think critically and sustain attention, memory, and understanding of theme over much longer texts. Full appreciation of texts requires noticing aspects of the writer's craft, including metaphor, simile, and symbolism. Many long texts have print in a much smaller font. Informational texts present complex ideas and may use language that is more technical. Topics are more often distant from students' experiences in time and place. Biographies provide a significant amount of historical information. Many focus on harsh themes. Other, longer biographies are told in narrative style but present complex themes.

Behaviors to Notice and Support

	Student's Name							
Understands and talks about complex themes, analyzing them and applying them to current life situations								
Understands many different perspectives that are encountered in fiction and nonfiction texts								
Evaluates both fiction and nonfiction texts for their authenticity and accuracy								
Deals with mature topics such as death, war, prejudice, and courage								
Thinks critically about and discusses the content of a literary work or the quality of writing								
Notices aspects of the writer's craft and looks at the text from a writer's point of view								
Sustains attention and thinking over the reading of texts that are long and have smaller fonts								
Tries new genres, topics, and authors, and is able to compare them with known genres, topics, and authors								
Makes connections across texts to notice an author's style or technique								
Understands symbolism in both realistic fiction and fantasy; discusses what symbols mean in terms of today's society								
Brings prior knowledge to bear in understanding literary references								
Learns technical language and concepts through reading								
Learns about self and others through reading, especially about societies that are different from one's own								

USING THE
GUIDED READING PROGRAM

Characteristics of Text

Texts at Level W have themes that explore the human condition, with the same kinds of social problems mentioned at earlier levels. Fiction and nonfiction texts present characters who suffer hardship and learn from it. The writing is sophisticated, with complex sentences, literary language, and symbolism. Texts vary in length; print is generally in a small font. Comprehending texts at this level will require awareness of social and political issues; through them, readers can learn to understand current social problems at deeper levels.

Fantasy includes science fiction as well as "high" fantasy that introduces heroic characters, questions, and contests between good and evil. Informational texts may present complex graphic information and require readers to possess a wide range of content knowledge and to understand all of the basic organizational structures for nonfiction. Narrative-style biographies include many details of their subjects' lives and prompt readers to make inferences about what motivated their achievements.

Behaviors to Notice and Support

Student's Name							
Sustains reading over longer and more complex texts; is not intimidated by varying layouts and styles of print							
Builds understanding of a wide variety of human problems							
Uses reading to expand awareness of people who are different from oneself							
Understands and learns from characters' experiences							
Learns about self and others through reading; actively seeks understanding of people different from oneself by culture, period of history, or other variation							
Deals with mature themes such as prejudice, war, death, survival, and poverty, and is able to discuss them in relation to one's own experiences							
Understands the complexities of human characters as they develop and change; discusses one's own point of view and relationship to characters							
Integrates understandings derived from graphic illustrations and the text							
Expands world knowledge through reading							
Flexibly and automatically uses tools such as glossary, references, index, credentials for authors, legends, charts, and diagrams							

USING THE
GUIDED READING PROGRAM

LEVEL X

Characteristics of Text

Texts at Level X include the same wide range of genres shown at previous levels, but the themes explored are increasingly mature. Fantasy depicts quests and the struggle between good and evil. High fantasy includes complex, extended symbolic narratives that require knowledge of previously read texts for full understanding. Readers are required to go substantially beyond the literal meaning of the text to construct a writer's implied meaning. In addition, texts require interpretation of theme and plot. In fiction texts, there may be many characters to follow and understand. There is a continuing increase in the sophistication of vocabulary, language, and topics. Nonfiction texts require extensive prior knowledge for full understanding. In addition, texts are designed to present a great deal of new knowledge, sometimes in a dense way. Graphic illustrations are helpful to readers but also require interpretation.

Behaviors to Notice and Support

	Student's Name						
Sustains attention over longer texts with more abstract, mature, and complex themes							
Notices, understands, and discusses a wide range of literary devices, such as flashbacks and stories within stories							
Deals with mature themes, such as family relationships, death, social injustice, and the supernatural							
Appreciates, understands, and discusses irony and satire							
Uses descriptive text as a way to understand settings and their importance to the plot or character development							
Discusses the setting as an element of the text, deciding whether it is important or unimportant							
Flexibly and automatically uses tools such as glossary, references, index, credentials for authors, legends, charts, and diagrams							
Notices aspects of the author's craft, including the way characters are described and presented as "real"							
Talks about the text in an analytic way, including finding specific evidence of the author's style							
Understands and is able to use the sophisticated, scholarly, and technical language that is found in informational texts							

Copyright © Scholastic Inc. All rights reserved.

GUIDED READING Nonfiction Focus 2nd Edition

Characteristics of Text 117

USING THE
GUIDED READING PROGRAM

Characteristics of Text

Books categorized as Level Y present subtle themes and complex plots. As with earlier levels, they include a whole range of social problems as themes, but more explicit details (for example, about death or prejudice) may be provided. Readers will need to bring considerable world experience and reading experience to their understanding of these more mature texts. Writers use symbolism, irony, satire, and other literary devices that require readers to think beyond the literal meaning of the text.

Books at Level Y include many more complex works of fantasy that depict hero figures and heroic journeys. Readers are required to discern underlying lessons and also to analyze texts for traditional elements. Informational texts explore an ever-widening world of history and science; topics require extensive prior knowledge of complex concepts, as well as vocabulary. Readers are required to gather new information from reading and synthesize it with their current knowledge. A wide range of critical reading skills are also required, so that students continuously evaluate the quality and objectivity of the texts they read.

Behaviors to Notice and Support

Student's Name							
Understands and discusses subtle and complex plots and themes							
Understands, discusses, and deals in a mature way with a wide range of social problems, including social injustice and tragedy							
Understands and discusses in a mature way texts that present explicit details of social problems							
Understands literary irony and satire as they are used to communicate big ideas							
Understands complex fantasy, entering into whole new worlds, and understands concepts in relation to the imagined setting							
Understands and discusses the fact that words can have multiple meanings in relation to the context in which they are used							
Flexibly and automatically uses tools such as glossary, references, index, credentials for authors, legends, charts, and diagrams							
Interprets events in light of the setting—time, place, and culture							
Engages in critical thinking about fiction and nonfiction texts							
Critically evaluates nonfiction texts for accuracy and presentation of information							

USING THE
GUIDED READING PROGRAM

Characteristics of Text

Level Z captures books that require reading strategies similar to those needed at lower levels, but which present such mature themes that readers simply need more experience to deal with them. Some students who are widely read may need this challenge. Some informational books present complex and technical information, sometimes within a denser text. Others deal with controversial social concepts and political issues that require readers to evaluate several points of view. Critical reading is essential, and readers often have to reevaluate and revise their own previously held beliefs. Historical texts have detailed accounts of periods of history that are less well known. Readers learn new ways of finding technical information, and encounter complex examples of the basic organizational structures for informational texts. Fiction texts explore a wide range of human themes, often with graphic details of hardship, violence, or tragedy. High fantasy presents heroic quests, symbolism, and complex characters, and involves the reader in considering the meaning of life.

Behaviors to Notice and Support

	Student's Name						
Sustains reading and understanding over much longer texts							
Deals with a great range of texts—from diaries to narratives to plays							
Switches easily from one genre to another, accessing knowledge of the structure and nature of the text while beginning to read							
Understands and discusses how a text "works" in terms of the writer's organization							
Deals with controversial social and political issues, seeing multiple perspectives							
Uses reading to gain technical knowledge in a wide variety of areas							
Understands the symbolism in heroic quests; applies concepts encountered in fantasy to today's life							
Flexibly and automatically uses tools such as glossary, references, index, credentials for authors, legends, charts, and diagrams							
Deals with and discusses in a mature way graphic details such as accounts of brutality, hardship, or violence							
Notices, understands, appreciates, and discusses literary devices							
Understands and appreciates complex language, archaic language, and cultural motifs							
Learns about epilogues, bibliographies, and forewords							
Builds information across the text, even when very unusual formats are used (for example, brief interviews with many characters)							
Fully understands the subtle differences between fiction and nonfiction							

READING LOG

LEVEL A

	Child's Name								
The Beach									
Count on Fish									
Hair									
In the Pond									
In the Woods									
Let's Go!									
Let's Make Soup									
The Little Panda									
Skippy Likes the Seasons									
Trucks									

LEVEL B

Can It Float?									
Count the Wheels									
Houses									
So Many Hats!									
Sounds on the Farm									
Sports									
Trees									
What Do You See?									
What's the Weather, Meg?									
Where Are Jack and Jill?									

LEVEL C

All Kinds of Boats									
Animal Tracks									
Be Happy!									
The Big Dinosaur Day!									
Birds and Beaks									
I Love Snow!									
Night									
Push! Pull! Move It!									
Spots or Stripes?									
A World of Flags!									

GUIDED READING Nonfiction Focus 2nd Edition

READING LOG

LEVEL D

	Child's Name								
At Home in a Shell									
Get Up and Go!									
Good for Us!									
In the Cold, Cold Sea									
Insect Countdown									
Just Write!									
Meet the Bears									
Penguins									
Snack Time									
What Kittens Need									

LEVEL E

Awake at Night									
City or Country?									
Horses Help									
In the Mountains									
Is This a Real Animal?									
Just in Time!									
On the Lake									
Pictures From Long Ago									
Tortillas									
What About Frogs?									

LEVEL F

Animals Are Living Things									
Animals Grow Up									
At Home in a Nest									
Big Rivers									
The Cows Are in the Corn									
Elephants									
The Enormous Turnip									
The Grass Grows									
Growing Pumpkins									
Where Do People Hike?									

GUIDED READING Nonfiction Focus 2nd Edition

READING LOG

	Child's Name								
LEVEL G									
Dinosaurs, Dinosaurs									
Fur, Feathers, or Fins?									
Hippo and Rabbit in Brave Like Me									
Munch! Crunch! Healthy Snacks									
Sharks									
The Three Little Pigs									
Way to Go!									
Whales									
What Can Insects Do?									
Who Needs Water?									
LEVEL H									
The 100th Day of School									
Color My World									
In the Jungle									
Life on a Coral Reef									
Plants We Eat									
Puppies									
Up, Down, and Around									
Up, Up, and Away: Toys That Fly									
What Goes Up . . .									
A World of Homes									
LEVEL I									
Baby Dolphin's First Day									
Blackout									
Butterflies									
Critters in Camouflage									
The Gobi Desert									
Kim's Trip to Hawaii									
My Five Senses									
The Shape of Things									
Two Eyes, a Nose, and a Mouth									
What the Dinosaurs Saw									

READING LOG

	Child's Name									
LEVEL J										
Go Ky a Flite										
A Monarch Butterfly's Life										
Only One										
Owl at Home										
Play Ball!										
Rap a Tap Tap: Here's Bojangles—Think of That!										
What's in Washington, D.C.?										
Wild Dogs										
Wonderful Worms										
Young Cam Jansen and the Lost Tooth										
LEVEL K										
10 Things I Can Do to Help My World										
A Boy Named Boomer										
Clifford for President										
A Dandelion's Life										
Have You Seen Birds?										
Monarch Butterflies										
Ruby Bridges Goes to School										
Sky Color										
Skyscrapers										
A Tree Is a Plant										
LEVEL L										
Biblioburro										
City Tales										
Elephants										
Frogs!										
A House for Hermit Crab										
Panda Kindergarten										
We Are Alike, We Are Different										
What Do Roots Do?										
What Do You Do With a Tail Like This?										
Winter Wonderland										

READING LOG

LEVEL M

	Child's Name								
Bat Loves the Night									
Chameleons Are Cool									
Dive! A Book of Deep-Sea Creatures									
An Eye for Color									
Frida									
From Seed to Plant									
Martin Luther King, Jr., and the March on Washington									
Throw Your Tooth on the Roof									
Two Bobbies: A True Story of Hurricane Katrina									
Why Do Dogs Bark?									

LEVEL N

Butterfly Boy									
Looking Closely in the Rain Forest									
The Magic School Bus Fixes a Bone									
My Light									
Odd Animal Helpers									
Owls									
The Paperboy									
Pet Heroes									
A Picture Book of Jesse Owens									
Surprising Swimmers									

LEVEL O

Apples to Oregon									
Beachcombing									
The Busy Body Book									
Coming to America: The Story of Immigration									
In the Garden With Dr. Carver									
Manfish									
Planets									
Rocks and Minerals									
Sonia Sotomayor: A Judge Grows in the Bronx									
Tell Me, Tree									

READING LOG

LEVEL P

Child's Name								
Amelia and Eleanor Go for a Ride								
The Boy Who Harnessed the Wind								
Girl Wonder								
Grandma's Gift								
If I Ran for President								
Life in the Ocean								
The Moon								
So You Want to Be an Inventor?								
Take a Giant Leap, Neil Armstrong!								
Wolverine vs. Tasmanian Devil								

LEVEL Q

Amazing Magnetism								
Away West								
Barnum's Bones								
Bugs								
The Camping Trip That Changed America								
Dinosaurs								
A Medieval Feast								
Playing to Win								
Testing the Ice								
WordGirl: Tobey or Consequences								

LEVEL R

Annie Sullivan and the Trials of Helen Keller								
The Buzz on Bees								
Everything Dolphin								
Horses								
Looking Like Me								
Luis Alvarez: Wild Idea Man								
Queen of the Track								
Sadako and the Thousand Paper Cranes								
The Trail of Tears								
Volcanoes								

READING LOG

Child's Name

LEVEL S

The Cod's Tale									
Dancing Home									
Helen Keller: Her Life in Pictures									
Lizards									
Louie: The Stray Who Was Saved									
Martin's Big Words									
Monster Hunt									
Nelson Mandela									
Neo Leo: The Ageless Ideas of Leonardo da Vinci									
A Thousand Cranes									

LEVEL T

Bad News for Outlaws									
Bill the Boy Wonder									
The Great Serum Race									
Hands Around the Library									
Ida B. Wells: Let the Truth Be Told									
Jackie Robinson: American Hero									
Looking at Lincoln									
Muscles									
My Librarian Is a Camel									
The Strongest Man in the World									

LEVEL U

Abe's Honest Words									
Around the World									
Boys Who Rocked the World									
Fearless									
Ghost Hunt									
I Dreamed of Flying Like a Bird									
The Life of Rice									
Titanic Sinks!									
Touch the Sky									
The Wright Brothers' First Flight									

GUIDED READING Nonfiction Focus 2nd Edition

READING LOG

Child's Name

LEVEL V

Dear America: So Far From Home								
Detector Dogs: Canines That Save Lives								
The Emperor's Silent Army								
Ice! The Amazing History of the Ice Business								
Into the Volcano								
King George: What Was His Problem?								
My Havana								
Rebel in a Dress: Adventurers								
Thunder From the Sea								
The Unexpected World of Nature								

LEVEL W

At Ellis Island: A History in Many Voices								
Baby Mammoth Mummy: Frozen in Time!								
Down to the Last Out								
Drawing From Memory								
Freedom Heroines								
Kubla Khan: The Emperor of Everything								
Tornado!								
Walt Whitman: Words for America								
Who Wants Pizza?								
Wonderstruck								

LEVEL X

Alexander Hamilton: The Outsider								
A Black Hole Is Not a Hole								
Case Closed?								
Fort Mose								
The Great Depression								
The Hidden Girl								
Lincoln Through the Lens								
The Lions of Little Rock								
The Odyssey of Flight 33								
UFOs: What Scientists Say May Shock You!								

GUIDED READING Nonfiction Focus 2nd Edition

READING LOG

LEVEL Y

	Child's Name								
10 Days: Abraham Lincoln									
Assassin									
Courage Has No Color									
Everything Ancient Egypt									
Gettysburg: The Graphic Novel									
How They Croaked									
Our Town									
We've Got a Job: The 1963 Birmingham Children's March									
Whatever Happened to the World of Tomorrow?									
World War II									

LEVEL Z

Ancient Rome									
Catching Fire									
The Dark Game									
Ghosts in the Fog									
Joseph Stalin									
The Monsters Are Due on Maple Street									
Mysterious Messages									
Teens at War									
Thoreau at Walden									
Unraveling Freedom									

ADDITIONAL LEVELED BOOKS AVAILABLE FROM SCHOLASTIC

Level A

Animals! Animals!
by Kate Sinclair

At Home on the Farm
by Bailey Carroll

Shapes
by Nat Gold

Summer Fun
by Sara Shapiro

We Like Fruit
by Millen Lee

What Can I Be?
by Cari Meister

Level B

Cats!
by Larry Dane Brimner

I Can Help!
by Hans Wilhelm

New Shoes
by Bridget Taylor

Reptiles
by Alex Ives

Toys
by Caryn Deer

Winter
by Janie Carr

Level C

At Work
by Ellen Geist

Bugs!
by Patricia and Fredrick McKissack

From Egg to Robin
by Susan Canizares and Betsey Chessen

I Can Run
by Gay Su Pinnell

I See Fish
by Don L. Curry

Rain
by Robert Kalan

Level D

Bugs! Bugs! Bugs!
by Bob Barner

Energy Is Everywhere
by June Young

Grow Flower, Grow!
by Lisa Bruce

Mud!
by Wendy Cheyette Lewison

Rainbows
by Karen Alexander

Level E

A Bean Plant Grows
by Vanessa York

A Box Can Be Many Things
by Dana Meachen Rau

I Am Water
by Jean Marzollo

Let's Go to the Zoo
by Cate Foley

Making Masks
by Karen Alexander

My Camera
by Andrew Carson

Level F

Firefighters A to Z
by Chris L. Demarest

Frog's Lunch
by Dee Lillegard

In the Small, Small Pond
by Denise Fleming

Shine, Sun!
by Carol Greene

Ten Black Dots
by Donald Crews

The White House
by Lloyd G. Douglas

Level G

Jane Goodall
by Jeannie Abrams

Just Like You and Me
by David Miller

Spiders Are Not Insects
by Allan Fowler

Trash and Treasure
by Vanessa York

Trees to Paper
by Inez Snyder

Your Brain
by Melvin and Gilda Berger

Level H

Amazing Wheat
by Katherine Phillipson

Building a House
by Byron Barton

I Am a Leaf
by Jean Marzollo

Let's Read About Martin Luther King, Jr.
by Courtney Baker

My Pigs
by Heather Miller

Shades of People
by Shelley Rotner and Sheila M. Kelly

ADDITIONAL LEVELED BOOKS AVAILABLE FROM SCHOLASTIC

Level I

A Day With a Mail Carrier
by Jan Kottke

Just Going to the Dentist
by Mercer Mayer

Landmarks U.S.A.
by Libby Brereton

Red-Eyed Tree Frog
by Joy Cowley

The Sun's Family of Planets
by Allan Fowler

Level J

Deep-Sea Explorers
by Vanessa York

How Kittens Grow
by Millicent E. Selsam

Lewis and Clark
by Kate Sinclair

Looking at Maps and Globes
by Carmen Bredeson

Meet the Monkeys and the Apes
by Libby Brereton

On the Lake
by Liane Onish

Level K

All About Things People Do
by Melanie and Chris Rice

Amazing Whales!
by Sarah L. Thomson

Chickens Aren't the Only Ones
by Ruth Heller

Follow the Money
by Loreen Leedy

Roadwork
by Sally Sutton

Level L

Cam Jansen and the Mystery of the Babe Ruth Baseball
by David Adler

Hibernation
by Tori Kosara

Rain Forest
by Anne Miranda

Spiders
by Gail Gibbons

What Makes a Magnet?
by Franklyn M. Branley

Level M

Boom!
by Howard Gutner

California or Bust!
by Judith Bauer Stamper

Chrysanthemum
by Kevin Henkes

Everybody Cooks Rice
by Norah Dooley

Owls, Bats, Wolves and Other Nocturnal Animals
by Kris Hirschmann

Yellowstone National Park
by David Petersen

Level N

The Cloud Book
by Tomie dePaola

Endangered Animals
by Lynn M. Stone

How Is a Crayon Made?
by Oz Charles

Louis Braille: The Boy Who Invented Books for the Blind
by Margaret Davidson

Remembering the Titanic
by Frieda Wishinsky

Voting
by Sarah De Capua

Level O

Amazing Tigers!
by Sarah L. Thomson

Desert Life
by Rachel Mann

Donner Party
by Tod Olson

I Wonder Why Snakes Shed Their Skins
by Amanda O'Neill

A Picture Book of Sojourner Truth
by David A. Adler

Take a Stand, Rosa Parks!
by Peter and Connie Roop

Level P

Biggest, Strongest, Fastest
by Steve Jenkins

Let's Drive, Henry Ford!
by Peter and Connie Roop

The Magic School Bus Has a Heart
by Anne Capeci, S.I. and Carolyn Bracken

Making Money for Kids
by Steven Otfinoski

Tarantula vs. Scorpion
by Jerry Pallotta

A Whale Is Not a Fish
by Melvin Berger

Level Q

Fabulous Facts About the 50 States
by Wilma S. Ross

If You Lived With the Hopi
by Anne Kamma

If Your Name Was Changed at Ellis Island
by Ellen Levine

The Story of George Washington Carver
by Eva Moore

The Story of Muhammad Ali
by Leslie Garrett

Level R

And Then What Happened, Paul Revere?
by Jean Fritz

The Brain
by Seymour Simon

Can It Rain Cats and Dogs?
by Melvin and Gilda Berger

Journey to Ellis Island
by Carol Bierman

The Tortoise Shell and Other African Stories
by Geof Smith

Level S

Bessie Coleman
by Bruce Brager

The Chicago Fire
by Howard Gutner

Eureka! It's Television
by Jeanne and Robert Bendick

In the Line of Fire: Eight Women War Spies
by George Sullivan

In the Year of the Boar and Jackie Robinson
by Betty Bao Lord

Mystery Math
by David A. Adler

Level T

The Big Lie
by Isabella Leitner

Bonanza Girl
by Patricia Beatty

The Girl Who Chased Away Sorrow
by Ann Turner

The Story of Levi's
by Michael Burgan

Volcano: The Eruption and Healing of Mount St. Helens
by Patricia Lauber

Where Are the Wolves?
by Rebecca Motil

Level U

America at War: Vietnam
by John Perritano

First Ladies
by Beatrice Gormley

Golden Games
by Stella Zemanski

Hoang Anh: A Vietnamese-American Boy
by Diane Hoyt-Goldsmith

Rosa Parks: My Story
by Rosa Parks with Jim Haskins

The Story of My Life
by Helen Keller

Level V

1000 Facts About Space
by Pam Beasant

Eleanor Roosevelt
by Wiley Blevins

Get on Board: The Story of the Underground Railroad
by Jim Haskins

How I Came to Be a Writer
by Phyllis Reynolds Naylor

Rocks and Minerals
by Dan Green

Under Wraps
by Meish Goldish

Level W

The Adventures of Ulysses
by Bernard Evslin

The First Woman Doctor
by Rachel Baker

Sea Otter Rescue
by Roland Smith

The Skin I'm In
by Sharon Flake

Titanic: Young Survivors
by Allan Zullo

You Want Women to Vote, Lizzie Stanton?
by Jean Fritz

ADDITIONAL **LEVELED BOOKS** AVAILABLE FROM SCHOLASTIC

Level X

Anne Frank: Beyond the Diary
by Ruud van der Rol and Rian Verhoeven

The Battle of Riptide
by EJ Altbacker

Bully for You, Teddy Roosevelt
by Jean Fritz

Feathers
by Jacqueline Woodson

Sarah Bishop
by Scott O'Dell

Summer of Fire
by Patricia Lauber

Level Y

Blizzard!
by Jim Murphy

Castle
by David Macaulay

The Colorado River
by Patricia Lauber

The Day Martin Luther King, Jr. Was Shot
by Jim Haskins

Seeing Earth From Space
by Patricia Lauber

Tales of Real Escape
by Paul Dowswell

Level Z

City: A Story of Roman Planning and Construction
by David Macaulay

The Day the Women Got the Vote
by George Sullivan

Great Escapes of World War II
by George Sullivan

The History of Emigration From China and Southeast Asia
by Katherine Prior

Triumph on Everest
by Broughton Coburn

Dear Family Member:

Your child is becoming a skilled independent reader! And the guided reading books that your reader will bring home are designed to help in this process.

As part of the *Scholastic Guided Reading Program,* your child will participate in small groups and will receive individualized instruction to develop fluency, oral language, vocabulary, phonics, comprehension, and writing skills. In addition, your child will bring home enjoyable, level-appropriate selections and stories that will help to ensure his or her success as an independent reader.

Here are some suggestions for helping your child before, during, and after reading:

Before

- Look at the book cover with your child. Together, review the photographs or illustrations in the book. Ask your child to predict what the selection will be about.

- Discuss what you and your child might already know about the topic of the book you are about to read.

- If your child is a beginning reader, echo-read the story or selection with your child by reading a line first and having your child read it after you. If your child is a more skilled reader, periodically stop and ask questions.

During

- If your child does not recognize a word right away, help him or her to focus on the familiar letters and spelling patterns in the word. Guide your child to think about other words that look like the unfamiliar word.

- Encourage your child to use phonics and decoding skills to sound out any new, unfamiliar words. If necessary, provide the word if your child struggles.

- Encourage your child to read with expression and to enjoy reading!

After

- Encourage your child to reread the selection to develop confidence. If the book is long, reread a few sections or chapters. Perhaps your child could read the book to other family members or friends.

- Discuss the book with your child. Ask questions such as: *What interesting facts did you learn? What were your favorite parts?*

- Have your child keep a journal of favorite books and interesting words in those books. Your child might also like to write about the book in this journal.

Have fun with this reading experience and your child will have fun, too!

Sincerely,

Estimado padre o tutor:

Su niño está en el proceso de convertirse en un lector hábil e independiente. Los libros de lectura guiada que su niño llevará a casa han sido concebidos para ayudar en este proceso.

Como parte del Programa de Lectura Guiada de Scholastic, su niño participará en grupos pequeños y recibirá instrucción individualizada con el objetivo de desarrollar la fluidez, el lenguaje oral, el vocabulario, la fonética, la comprensión y las destrezas de escritura. Además, su niño llevará a casa lecturas amenas y apropiadas a su nivel, que le servirán para garantizar su éxito como lector independiente.

Éstas son algunas sugerencias para ayudar a su niño antes, durante y después de la lectura:

Antes

- Observe con su niño la cubierta del libro. Repasen juntos las ilustraciones o fotografías del libro. Pídale a su niño predecir de qué tratará el cuento o la selección que van a leer.

- Comenten lo que usted y su niño ya sepan sobre el tema del libro que van a leer.

- Si su niño es un lector principiante, lea usted primero una línea y pídale que lea esa misma línea después. Si su niño es un lector más avanzado, haga una pausa de vez en cuando para hacerle preguntas.

Durante

- Si a su niño le resulta difícil reconocer alguna palabra, ayúdelo a fijarse en las letras y patrones ortográficos con los que esté familiarizado. Guíe a su niño en la búsqueda de otras palabras que se parezcan a la palabra desconocida.

- Anime a su niño a usar la fonética y las destrezas de decodificación para leer en voz alta cualquier palabra nueva o desconocida. Si su niño tiene dificultades para hacerlo de manera independiente, lea usted la palabra.

- Anime a su niño a leer de manera expresiva y a disfrutar de la lectura.

Después

- Anime a su niño a volver a leer el cuento o la selección para que gane confianza como lector. Si el libro es demasiado largo, vuelva a leer algunas de las secciones o pasajes favoritos. También puede pedirle que lea el cuento a otros familiares o amigos.

- Comente con su niño el cuento o la selección. Hágale preguntas como las siguientes: *¿Qué hecho o dato importante aprendiste leyendo este libro? ¿Qué partes te gustaron más? ¿Qué personajes son tus favoritos? ¿Por qué?*

- Pídale que lleve un récord de sus selecciones y cuentos favoritos, así como de las palabras interesantes que encuentre en los mismos. También, puede llevar un diario con comentarios sobre los libros.

Disfrute de la lectura. ¡Su niño, de seguro, también disfrutará!

Atentamente,

TECHNOLOGY

Information on Guided Reading and how to implement it in your classroom is provided at **www.scholastic.com.** In addition, the site contains numerous teacher, student, and parent resources related to books in the Guided Reading Program. Use these resources for independent and group extension activities.

teacher resources

student activities

Scholastic Reading Counts! quizzes are available for many of the titles in this Guided Reading Program. These quizzes can be used to monitor student comprehension and make decisions about each student's instructional needs.

Skills & Strategies Chart

Level	Title	Author	Genre/Text Type	Content Area	Comprehension Analyze Text	Writing Options	Phonics/Word Study	Themes/Ideas	Technology
A	Beach, The	Ives, Alex	Informational Text Picture Book	Science Earth Science: Seashore	recognize patterned text	label (Inf./Exp.) sentence (Inf./Exp.)	naming words initial consonant s	studying nature; exploring relationships	http://water.epa.gov/learn/kids/beachkids/
A	Count on Fish	Tree, Rebecca	Informational Text Picture Book	Math Math: Counting	use picture clues	chart (Inf./Exp.) story (Narrative)	identify parts of a book number words	practicing mathematics; studying animals	http://www.scholastic.com/earlylearner/parentandchild/math/count.htm
A	Hair	Wilton, Briar	Informational Text Picture Book	Social Studies Culture: Hair	identify key details in photos/text	group list (Inf./Exp.) group book (Narrative)	develop print awareness phonogram -ed	comparing and contrasting hair types; learning words that describe	http://kidshealth.org/kid/htbw/hair.html#
A	In the Pond	Hearn, Carol	Informational Text Picture Book	Science Animal Habitats: Pond	compare information in photos and text	draw and label (Inf./Exp.) patterned text (Inf./Exp.)	develop print awareness initial consonants	exploring nature; learning about environments	http://www.ypte.org.uk/environmental/ponds/84
A	In the Woods	Charles, Stella	Informational Text Picture Book	Science Animal Habitats: Woods	locate information	draw and write (Inf./Exp.) sentence (Inf./Exp.)	develop print awareness high-frequency words	exploring nature; analyzing nature photography	http://kids.nationalgeographic.com/kids/animals/creaturefeature/raccoons/
A	Let's Go!	Theo, Diane	Informational Text Picture Book	Social Studies Kinds of Transportation	recognize patterned text	draw and label (Narrative) sentence (Narrative)	develop print awareness naming words	identifying things that go; comparing things that go	http://pbskids.org/barney/children/games/transportation_game.html
A	Let's Make Soup	Gibbs, Jephson	Fantasy Picture Book		describe story events	recipe (Inf./Exp.) description (Inf./Exp.)	develop print awareness words that name more than one	cooking is fun; following a recipe	http://www.scholastic.com/ispy/games/bingo.htm
A	Little Panda, The	Noonan, Joe	Informational Text Picture Book	Science Life Science: Baby Animals	compare information in photos/text	draw and label (Inf./Exp.) write a fact (Inf./Exp.)	develop print awareness action words	identifying baby animals; identifying wild animals	http://kids.sandiegozoo.org/animals/mammals/giant-panda
A	Skippy Likes the Seasons	Carroll, Bailey	Informational Text Picture Book	Science Life Science: Seasons	identify key details in photos/text	draw and label (Inf./Exp.) sentence (Inf./Exp.)	develop print awareness initial sounds	enjoying the companionship of a dog; learning about the seasonal changes	www.scholastic.com/clifford/play/seasonalstickers/stickers.htm
A	Trucks	Craft, Jane	Fantasy Picture Book		use picture clues	draw and label (Inf./Exp.) describe (Inf./Exp.)	develop print awareness initial sounds	spending time with family; exploring one's neighborhood	http://www.sparky.org/firetruck/index.htm
B	Can It Float?	Carroll, Bailey	Informational Text Picture Book	Science Physical Science: Things That Float	compare and contrast	description (Inf./Exp.) sentence (Inf./Exp.)	develop print awareness initial sounds	comparing and contrasting; identifying living and nonliving things	http://www.pbslearningmedia.org/resource/lsps07.sci.phys.matter.cgboatfloat/a-boat-that-floats/
B	Count the Wheels	Daniels, Felix	Informational Text Picture Book	Math Math: Grouping	compare and contrast details	chart (Inf./Exp.) answers (Inf./Exp.)	develop print awareness number words	counting; grouping like things	www.pbskids.org/curiousgeorge/busyday/allie/
B	Houses	Frazier, Whit	Informational Text Picture Book	Social Studies Homes/Colors	identify key details in photos/text	write an opinion (Opinion) list (Inf./Exp.)	develop print awareness describing words	examining architecture; understanding design	http://www.abcya.com/abcya_paint.htm
B	So Many Hats!	Ryder, Charles	Informational Text Picture Book	Social Studies Jobs	identify key details in photos	draw and label (Inf./Exp.) sentence (Narrative)	develop print awareness words with short vowels: a, i	exploring equipment for particular jobs; imagining doing particular jobs	http://kids.usa.gov/jobs/a-z-list/index.shtml
B	Sounds on the Farm	Ives, Alex	Informational Text Picture Book	Science Classifying Animals	use picture and context clues	draw and label (Inf./Exp.) state an opinion (Opinion)	develop print awareness action words	learning words that name animal sounds; exploring animal habitats	http://www.activityvillage.co.uk/farm-animals
B	Sports	Wolfe, Jessica	Informational Text Picture Book	Social Studies Sports	ask and answer questions	draw and label (Inf./Exp.) story (Narrative)	high-frequency words action words	identifying particular sports; comparing and contrasting balls used in sports	http://pbskids.org/video/
B	Trees	Mitchell, Sara	Informational Text Picture Book	Science Life Science: Parts of Trees	understand structure	chart (Inf./Exp.) story (Narrative)	develop print awareness words with long vowel e	exploring nature; learning about the environment	http://www.arborday.org/kids/carly/lifeofatree/
B	What Do You See?	Flaherty, Heather	Informational Text Picture Book	Math Math: Sorting	use photos to answer questions	draw and label (Opinion) write an answer (Inf./Exp.)	develop print awareness words with long vowel e	seeing relationships between animals; recognizing question marks and questions in text	http://kids.sandiegozoo.org/activities/zoodles/create
B	What's the Weather, Meg?	Smith, Janie	Fantasy Picture Book		ask and answer questions	chart (Inf./Exp.) list (Inf./Exp.)	syllables phonemes	planning ahead for weather; using weather words	www.theweatherchannelkids.com
B	Where Are Jack and Jill?	Rothman, Cynthia	Fantasy Picture Book		compare and contrast	group story (Narrative) sentences (Narrative)	develop print awareness initial consonant j	using clues to identify a place; learning words that tell about position	http://www.meddybemps.com/opposites/FullEmpty.html
C	All Kinds of Boats	Noonan, Joe	Informational Text Picture Book	Social Studies Transportation: Boats	compare photos and text	answer a question (Opinion) list (Inf./Exp.)	initial consonant b long o spelled oa	identifying different kinds of boats; learning about opposites	http://www.marinersmuseum.org/crabtree/timeline
C	Animal Tracks	Parker, Richard	Informational Text Picture Book	Science Life Science: Classifying Animals	use picture clues	sentence (Inf./Exp.) story (Narrative)	develop print awareness words with long e: e, e, ea	recognizing animal names; using pictures to make predictions	http://www.survival.org.au/tracking.php
C	Be Happy!	Dale, Cooper	Informational Text Picture Book	Social Studies Health/Happiness	compare and contrast ideas	sentence (Inf./Exp.) story (Narrative)	words with -ing long a spelled a_e	identifying different activities that children like; learning words for things children do	http://www.scholastic.com/clifford/play/peekaboo/peekaboo.htm

* Titles are CCSS exemplar texts.

Level	Title	Author	Genre/Text Type	Content Area	Comprehension Analyze Text	Writing Options	Phonics/Word Study	Themes/Ideas	Technology
C	Big Dinosaur Day!, The	Lee, Julia	Realistic Fiction Picture Book		identify character/setting	extend story (Narrative) sentence (Inf./Exp.)	quotation marks contractions	pursuing your interests; putting needs before wants	http://www.mnh.si.edu/panoramas
C	Birds and Beaks	Wolfe, Jessica	Informational Text Picture Book	Science Life Science: Bird Adaptations	locate information	draw and label (Inf./Exp.) T-chart (Inf./Exp.)	develop print awareness describing words	comparing and contrasting; using text and photographs together to learn	http://www.fernbank.edu/Birding/bird_beaks.htm
C	I Love Snow!	Ives, Alex	Informational Text Picture Book	Science Earth Science: Snow	connect ideas in a text	sentence (Opinion) draw and label (Inf./Exp.)	develop print awareness sound of ow	learning about snow; identifying what people and animals can do in snow	http://www.starfall.com/n/holiday/snowman/play.htm
C	Night	Ryder, Charles	Informational Text Picture Book	Social Studies Geography: Paris/Night	identify key details in photos	chart (Inf./Exp.) picture (Inf./Exp.)	high-frequency words phonogram -ight	viewing Paris at night; thinking about what you see at night	http://geology.com/articles/satellite-photo-earth-at-night.shtml
C	Push! Pull! Move It!	Taylor, Bob	Informational Text Picture Book	Science Physical Science	connect ideas in a text	poster (Inf./Exp.) sentence (Inf./Exp.)	develop print awareness words with short vowels	finding the best way to move things; learning what the body can do	http://www.bbc.co.uk/schools/scienceclips/ages/5_6/pushes_pulls.shtml
C	Spots or Stripes?	Adley, Laurence	Informational Text Picture Book	Science/Math Life Science: Animal Patterns/Classifying	identify key details	description (Inf./Exp.) draw and label (Opinion)	develop print awareness phonogram -at	comparing and contrasting; learning about baby and adult animals	http://www.bigcats.com/upload_random.php
C	World of Flags!, A	Roman, Rebecca	Informational Text Picture Book	Social Studies World Culture: Flags	identify main topic and key details	draw and label (Inf./Exp.) dictionary (Inf./Exp.)	proper nouns high-frequency words	understanding that flags represent countries; learning words that describe colors and shapes	http://www.learninggamesforkids.com/geography_games/random_games/flags.shtml
D	At Home in a Shell	Jordan, Charlotte	Informational Text Picture Book	Science Life Science: Animals in a Shell	compare and contrast ideas	add a sentence (Narrative) fact (Inf./Exp.)	initial consonant h words with short e	exploring characteristics of a home; using photos to get information	http://animals.sandiegozoo.org/animals/turtle-tortoise
D	Get Up and Go!	Taylor, Bob	Informational Text	Health Exercise/Fitness	identify main topic and key details	dictionary (Inf./Exp.) draw/write (Inf./Exp.)	proper nouns final consonant sounds	playing outside is fun; recognizing ways to get up and go	http://pbskids.org/zoom/activities/games/
D	Good for Us!	Rothman, Cynthia	Fantasy Picture Book	Science	ask and answer questions	poster (Inf./Exp.) sentence (Opinion)	naming words consonant blend gr	choosing healthy snacks; sharing with friends	http://www.choosemyplate.gov/kids/
D	In the Cold, Cold Sea	Dana, Lucy	Informational Text Picture Book	Science Polar Animals/Habitat	understand text features	draw and write (Narrative) sentence (Inf./Exp.)	initial and final consonants long o spelled o	comparing and contrasting polar climate animals; thinking about where animals spend most of their time	http://climatekids.nasa.gov/arctic-animals/
D	Insect Countdown	Ives, Alex	Informational Text Picture Book	Science/Math Insects/Counting Down	use picture and context clues	countdown book (Inf./Exp.) group story (Narrative)	number and number words initial consonants	learning about what insects do; learning about how insects move	http://kids.sandiegozoo.org/animals
D	Just Write!	Quick, Joanna	Informational Text Picture Book	Language Arts Communication: Writing	connect ideas in a text	create a card (Inf./Exp.) answer a question (Inf./Exp.)	punctuation words with r-controlled vowels	people share thoughts in writing; writing is a way to express ideas	http://www.nhcs.net/parsley/curriculum/postal/FriendlyLetter.html
D	Meet the Bears	Stuart, Cynthia	Informational Text Picture Book	Science Life Science: Classifying Bears	ask and answer questions	sentence (Inf./Exp.) sentence (Opinion)	number words words that name more than one	comparing and contrasting bears; counting bear cubs	http://www.sandiegozoo.org/pandacam/gallery.html
D	Penguins	Worley, Amelia	Informational Text Picture Book	Science Life Science: Emperor Penguins	understand sequence of events	draw a picture (Inf./Exp.) story (Narrative)	pronoun: they words with long i	penguins are adapted to live in cold places; penguins can't fly, but they can swim fast	http://www.kidzone.ws/animals/penguins
D	Snack Time	Smith, Janie	Fantasy Picture Book		identify characters/settings/events	character (Narrative) write/place (Narrative)	quotation marks ending sounds	going into town for supplies; understanding where to go to buy snacks	http://www.healthykids.nsw.gov.au/
D	What Kittens Need	Parker, Emily	Informational Text Picture Book	Science Life Science: Pet Care	identify the main topic and key details	opinion piece (Opinion) story (Narrative)	phonogram -ay consonant blend: pl	valuing caring and love; knowing that animals need more than food	http://kids.nationalgeographic.com/kids/photos/gallery/cats
E	Awake at Night	Wolfe, Jessica	Informational Text Picture Book	Science Life Science: Nocturnal Animals	use context clues	story (Narrative) question/answer (Inf./Exp.)	action words with -ing long a spelled a_e	exploring animal activities; learning about animal habitats	http://teacher.scholastic.com/commclub/strangest_night_animals_activity/page-2.htm
E	City or Country?	Ellen, J. C.	Informational Text Picture Book	Social Studies Geography: City vs. Country	compare and contrast ideas	label (Inf./Exp.) opinion (Opinion)	long e spelled y hard and soft c	understanding social studies concepts; identifying relationships between people and places	http://www.britishcouncil.org/kids-print-houses.pdf
E	Horses Help	Cherrington, Janelle	Informational Text Picture Book	Social Studies History: Horses Help People	use information from photos and text	write reasons (Opinion) story (Narrative)	high-frequency words	comparing how humans use horses then and now; identifying how horses help us	www.sciencekids.co.nz/sciencefacts/animals/horse.html
E	In the Mountains	Eli, Beth	Informational Text Picture Book	Science Earth & Life Science: Mountain Animals	identify main topic and key details	story (Narrative) chart (Inf./Exp.)	one- and two-syllable words short a and long a	learning what animals need; people can live in the same places animals do	http://www.nps.gov/grsm/naturescience/animals.htm

* Titles are CCSS exemplar texts.

Level	Title	Author	Genre/Text Type	Content Area	Comprehension Analyze Text	Writing Options	Phonics/Word Study	Themes/Ideas	Technology
E	Is This a Real Animal?	Caryn, Jane	Informational Text Picture Book	Science Life Science: Animal Traits	understand words and phrases	describe (Inf./Exp.) opinion (Opinion)	short vowels syllables	learning about unusual animals; identifying animal characteristics	www.sciencedump.com/content/collection-beautiful-strange-animals
E	Just in Time!	Worley, Amelia	Fantasy Picture Book		distinguish between fantasy and reality	description (Narrative) chart (Inf./Exp.)	high-frequency words words with short u	recognizing times on a clock; describing a sequence of tasks	http://www.arkive.org/red-squirrel/sciurus-vulgaris/image-A4239.html
E	On the Lake	Jones, Clara	Informational Text Picture Book	Science Physical Science: Water	ask and answer questions	description (Inf./Exp.) email (Narrative)	words with long a words that name more than one	observing details; recognizing that people and animals share lakes	http://pbskids.org/sid/fablab_weathersurprise.html
E	Pictures From Long Ago	Tree, Rebecca	Informational Text Picture Book	Social Studies History: Things Change Over Time	use information from photos and text	description (Inf./Exp.) lists (Inf./Exp.)	long a spelled ai words with -ing	exploring how people and things change over time; examining historical photographs	http://www.pbs.org/wgbh/amex/telephone/gallery/gallery1.html
E	Tortillas	Gonzáles-Jensen, Margarita	Realistic Fiction Picture Book		identify words/phrases	label (Narrative) sentence (Narrative)	beginning and ending sounds consonant blends	exploring family traditions; identifying repeated text	http://ft.webmd.com/jr/food/article/cheese-tortilla-recipe
E	What About Frogs?	Michaels, L. Ben	Informational Text Picture Book	Science Life Science: Frog Traits	recognize questions and answers	story (Narrative) new page (Inf./Exp.)	naming words consonant blends	using photos to get information; learning about animal habitats	https://www.nwf.org/Kids/Ranger-Rick/Animals/Amphibians-and-Reptiles/Frogs.aspx
F	Animals Are Living Things	Drew, Lucy	Informational Text Picture Book	Science Life Science: Identifying Living Things	identify main idea and key details	description (Inf./Exp.) fact cards (Inf./Exp.)	verb ending -ing	seeing animals care for their young; seeing the stages in animal growth	http://pbskids.org/dragonflytv/show/babyanimals.html
F	Animals Grow Up	Nelson, May	Informational Text Picture Book	Science Life Cycles: Animals Grow Up	use text features	chart (Inf./Exp.) narrative (Narrative)	words with digraphs	studying animal habitats; comparing and contrasting	http://www.sandiegozoo.org/whatsnew/
F	At Home in a Nest	Wilton, Briar	Informational Text Picture Book	Science Life Science: Nests and Birds	understand words and phrases	dialogue (Narrative) labeled drawing (Inf./Exp.)	consonant blend: st r-controlled vowel: ir	finding amazing things in nature; learning how people and animals live	http://cams.allaboutbirds.org/
F	Big Rivers	Ryder, Charles	Informational Text Picture Book	Social Studies Geography: Using Rivers	connect ideas in a text	draw and label (Inf./Exp.) story (Narrative)	words with short i initial consonant blends: tr, pl	describing animals; seeing animals in their habitats	www.rivers.gov/kids/funfacts.html
F	Cows Are in the Corn, The	Young, James	Humorous Fiction Picture Book		describe story elements	rhyme (Narrative) extend the story (Narrative)	context clues plural words	learning about jobs on a farm; identifying problem and solution	http://www.agclassroom.org/kids/ag_facts.htm
F	Elephants	Noonan, Joe	Informational Text Picture Book	Science Life Science: Animal Behavior	use information from photos and text	description (Inf./Exp.) fact cards (Inf./Exp.)	words with short u	identifying how animals meet their basic needs; analyzing how animals grow and survive	http://kids.sandiegozoo.org/animals/mammals/african-elephant#animals
F	Enormous Turnip, The	McBeath, Bridie	Folk Tale Picture Book		use picture clues	opinion piece (Opinion) retell a story (Narrative)	words with ou consonant blends	recognizing too much of a good thing; recognizing that size doesn't always matter	http://www.bbc.co.uk/schoolradio/subjects/collectiveworship/collectiveworship_stories/SEAL/relationships_enormous_turnip
F	Grass Grows, The	Gibbs, Jephson	Informational Text Picture Book	Science Life Science: Plants	locate information	game (Narrative) concept web (Inf./Exp.)	consonant blend: gr words with oo	identifying plants in the grass family; learning different ways people use grasses	http://www.sciencetoymaker.org/grassyHead/GrassyHead.pdf
F	Growing Pumpkins	Ives, Alex	Informational Text Picture Book	Science Life Science: How Pumpkins Grow	compare information in text and photos	diagrams (Inf./Exp.) favorite fact (Inf./Exp.)	long vowel i spelled i_e words into syllables	observing the stages in growth; distinguishing ripe from unripe	http://www.sciencekids.co.nz/sciencefacts/food/pumpkins.html
F	Where Do People Hike?	Roberts, Dee	Informational Text Picture Book	Social Studies Geography	recognize questions and answers	opinion (Opinion) write questions (Inf./Exp.)	words with oo words that name more than one	appreciating nature; exploring the outdoors	http://hikesafe.com/index.php?page=kids
G	Dinosaurs, Dinosaurs	Barton, Byron	Informational Text Picture Book	Science Life Science: Dinosaur Traits	identify main topic and key details	draw and label (Inf./Exp.) fact (Inf./Exp.)	context clues antonyms	learning about the past; comparing and contrasting animals	http://pbskids.org/dinosaurtrain/games/fieldguide.html
G	Fur, Feathers, or Fins?	Carroll, Bailey	Informational Text Picture Book	Science Life Science: Classifying Animals	identify main idea and key details	chart (Inf./Exp.) fact (Inf./Exp.)	long o spelled o	learning about animal adaptations; sorting animals based on skin covering	http://nationalzoo.si.edu/animals/photogallery/default.cfm
G	Hippo and Rabbit in Brave Like Me	Mack, Jeff	Fantasy Picture Book		describe story elements	opinion (Opinion) draw a scene (Narrative)	contractions	taking a bath; solving a problem	www.jeffmack.com/chapter_books.html
G	Munch! Crunch! Healthy Snacks	Michaels, David	Informational Text Picture Book	Science Health	understand categorization	flash cards (Inf./Exp.) story (Narrative)	consonant digraphs	learning that healthy food tastes good; appreciating the different colors that snacks come in	http://www.foodchamps.org
G	Sharks	Berger, Melvin and Gilda	Informational Text Picture Book	Science Life Science: Sharks	identify key details	Venn diagram (Inf./Exp.) favorite (Opinion)	final consonants	knowing habitats of sharks; learning how real sharks differ from fantasy sharks	http://www.kidzone.ws/sharks/facts1.htm
G	Three Little Pigs, The	Banks, Emily	Folk Tale Picture Book		describe characters/events	make a plan (Inf./Exp.) extend the story (Narrative)	plural words ending sounds	making a plan; retelling a traditional tale	http://video.nhptv.org/video/2238439827/

* Titles are CCSS exemplar texts.

Level	Title	Author	Genre/Text Type	Content Area	Comprehension Analyze Text	Writing Options	Phonics/Word Study	Themes/Ideas	Technology
G	Way to Go!	Thomas, Annie	Informational Text Picture Book	Social Studies Transportation	ask and answer questions	draw and label (Inf./Exp.) story (Narrative)	words with long o words that tell about location	discovering the places people can travel; comparing and contrasting methods of transportation	http://pbskids.org/designsquad/build/4-wheel-balloon-car/
G	Whales	Berger, Melvin and Gilda	Informational Text Picture Book	Science Life Science: Whales	use information from photos and text	draw and label (Inf./Exp.) story (Narrative)	words with long e suffix -est	identifying features of whales; learning about baby whales	www.nmfs.noaa.gov/pr/education/whales.htm
G	What Can Insects Do?	Rothman, Cynthia	Informational Text Picture Book	Science Life Science: Insects	understand text features	draw and label (Inf./Exp.) complete a sentence (Narrative)	consonant blends action words	connecting animal parts with movement; exploring nature	http://www.nwf.org/Kids/Ranger-Rick/Animals/Insects-and-Arthropods/What-Good-Are-Bugs.aspx
G	Who Needs Water?	Rothman, Cynthia	Informational Text Picture Book	Science Life Science: Living Things Need Water	relate key details to the main idea	description (Inf./Exp.) narrative (Narrative)	short vowels nouns and verbs	studying the needs of living things; studying animal survival	http://www.nwf.org/Kids/Ranger-Rick-Jr/Bear-Video.aspx
H	100th Day of School, The	Medearis, Angela Shelf	Realistic Fiction Picture Book	Social Studies Living	identify words and phrases	sentence (Narrative) draw and write (Narrative)	consonant blends with s plural words	identifying classroom activities; understanding milestones	http://pbskids.org/cyberchase/math-games
H	Color My World	Carroll, Bailey	Informational Text Picture Book	Science Physical Science/Colors	distinguish between text and photos	color list (Inf./Exp.) write/color (Inf./Exp.)	articles a and an commas and ellipses	recognizing objects associated with certain colors; appreciating the beauty of colors	http://www.artprojectsforkids.org/2012/08/color-wheel-for-elementary-students.html
H	In the Jungle	Drew, Lucy	Informational Text Picture Book	Social Studies Habitats: Jungle	identify main idea and key details	opinion (Opinion) chart (Inf./Exp.)	long a spelled a_e words that end with -le	studying animal habitats; learning about animal species	http://www.sheppardsoftware.com/preschool/animals/jungle/animaljunglemovie.htm
H	Life on a Coral Reef	Berger, Melvin and Gilda	Informational Text Picture Book	Science Life Science: Underwater Animals/Life-forms	use information from photos and text	label (Inf./Exp.) express opinion (Opinion)	words with or digraph sh	learning about underwater animals; identifying unfamiliar life forms	http://www.kidsdiscover.com/blog/spotlight/coral-reefs/
H	Plants We Eat	York, Vanessa	Informational Text Photo Essay	Science Life Science/Plants	understand sequence of events	chart (Inf./Exp.) recipe (Inf./Exp.)	dialogue nouns	recognizing a sequence of steps; learning where food comes from	http://pbskids.org/sid/fablab_vegetableplanting.html
H	Puppies	Sexton, Colleen	Informational Text Chapter Book	Science Life Science	understand words and phrases	caption (Inf./Exp.) sequence chart (Inf./Exp.)	plurals words ending in -ly	naming animal actions; identifying animal needs	www.pbskids.org/itsmylife/family/pets/article/.html
H	Up, Down, and Around	Ayres, Katherine	Informational Text Picture Book	Science/Math Plant Growth/Location	use picture details	sentence (Narrative) menu (Inf./Exp.)	words with ow and ou syllables	identifying directions; understanding food sources	http://ahgarden.cowplex.com/Virtual_Garden
H	Up, Up, and Away: Toys That Fly	Scott, Janine	Informational Text Picture Book	Science Physical Science: Flight	use text features	experiment (Inf./Exp.) description (Inf./Exp.)	spellings of long i consonant blends	naming kinds of toys; examining wind and gravity	http://www.youtube.com/watch?v=zioRQGsqCEg
H	What Goes Up...	Mitchell, Sara	Fantasy Picture Book	Social Studies Solving a Problem/Cause and Effect	describe story events	storyboard (Narrative) opinion (Opinion)	identify double consonants	understanding gravity; exploring friendship	http://www.iptv.org/kids/story.cfm/video/pbskids_2011111_gravity/video
H	World of Homes, A	Baker, Amy	Informational Text Picture Book	Social Studies Culture/Building Materials	ask and answer questions	label (Inf./Exp.) complete sentences (Inf./Exp.)	initial consonant blends short-vowel sounds	understanding different ways of life; learning about people and homes around the world	http://www.hgpho.to/wfest/house/house-e.html
I	Baby Dolphin's First Day	Roop, Peter and Roop, Connie	Informational Text Picture Book	Science Life Science: Dolphins/Caring for Young	connect ideas in a text	advice (Opinion) description (Inf./Exp.)	consonant digraphs	understanding how wild animals care for their young; appreciating the intelligence of dolphins	http://www.smithsonianmag.com/video/Under-the-Sea-with-Dolphins.html
I	Blackout	Rocco, John	Realistic Fiction Graphic Novel		describe characters	cartoon (Narrative) sounds (Narrative)	onomatopoeia	learning about what happens during a blackout; learning about city living	http://kids.saveonenergy.ca/en/what-is-electricity/
I	Butterflies	Neye, Emily	Informational Text Picture Book	Science Life Science: Life Cycles of Butterflies	understand sequence	flow chart (Inf./Exp.) review (Opinion)	compound words plurals	comparing butterflies and moths; identifying insects	http://kids.sandiegozoo.org/animals/insects/butterfly
I	Critters in Camouflage	Alexander, Karen	Informational Text Picture Book	Science Animal Traits/Adaptation	identify key details in photos and text	draw and describe (Inf./Exp.) description (Inf./Exp.)	words with long a spelled a_e homophones	describing the appearance of living things; identifying different animals	www.abc.net.au/beasts/playground/camouflage.htm
I	Gobi Desert, The	Alexander, Karen	Informational Text Picture Book	Social Studies Desert Habitat: Gobi	distinguish between photos and text	letter (Narrative) fact card (Inf./Exp.)	pronouns	understanding world geography; seeing how people live in harsh climates	http://www.sandiegozoo.org/animalbytes/t-camel.html
I	Kim's Trip to Hawaii	Cohen, Carlie	Realistic Fiction Picture Book		identify setting	poster (Opinion) letter (Narrative)	possessives: words with 's proper nouns	spending time with family; enjoying vacation	www.gohawaii.com/big-island/about
I	* My Five Senses	Aliki	Informational Text Picture Book	Science Life Science: Identifying Five Senses	use context and picture clues	sentences (Inf./Exp.) class book (Narrative)	words with oo verbs with -ing	identifying the five senses; learning words related to the five senses	http://kidshealth.org/kid/closet/experiments/experiment_main.html
I	Shape of Things, The	Dodds, Dayle Ann	Informational Text Picture Book	Math Real-World Shapes	identify information in pictures/words	draw and label (Inf./Exp.) complete a verse (Narrative)	sound/spelling correspondence	understanding our world; appreciating poetry	http://pbskids.org/games/shapes.html
I	Two Eyes, a Nose, and a Mouth	Intrater, Roberta Grobel	Informational Text Picture Book	Social Studies Culture: Diversity of Facial Features	connect ideas in a text	description (Inf./Exp.) story (Narrative)	adjectives	exploring similarities and differences; comparing and contrasting	http://www.alphabetikids.com/

* Titles are CCSS exemplar texts.

Level	Title	Author	Genre/Text Type	Content Area	Comprehension Analyze Text	Writing Options	Phonics/ Word Study	Themes/Ideas	Technology
I	What the Dinosaurs Saw	Schlein, Miriam	Informational Text Picture Book	Science Life Science: Dinosaurs	use information from illustrations and text	description (Inf./Exp.) riddle (Inf./Exp.)	inflectional ending -ing	comparing and contrasting then and now; counting	http://kids.sandiegozoo.org/animals/
J	Go Ky a Flite	Cowley, Joy	Fantasy Picture Book		understand cause and effect	how-to guide (Inf./Exp.) story (Narrative)	context clues	recognizing the effects of actions; helping others	http://robotic.media.mit.edu
J	Monarch Butterfly's Life, A	Himmelman, John	Informational Text Picture Book	Science Life Cycles: Monarch Butterfly	recognize sequence	story (Narrative) poster (Inf./Exp.)	common prefixes	understanding seasonal changes; learning scientific terms	http://video.pbs.org/video/1063682334/
J	Only One	Harshman, Marc	Informational Text Picture Book	Math Parts of a Whole/ Counting Objects	use context and picture clues	another page (Inf./Exp.) sequel (Narrative)	two-syllable words	reading numerals; recognizing individuality	http://www.barbaragarrison.com/collagraphJumpPage.html
J	Owl at Home	Lobel, Arnold	Fantasy Short Stories		describe characters/events	letter (Narrative) graphic organizer (Narrative)	compound words	recognizing exaggeration; recognizing the importance of feeling safe	http://e-learningforkids.org/Courses/EN/S0801/login.htm
J	Play Ball!	York, Vanessa	Informational Text Picture Book	Social Studies Sports: Baseball	connect ideas in a text	sports article (Narrative) want ad (Inf./Exp.)	multiple-meaning words words with suffix -er	examining recreational activities; appreciating outdoor activities	http://www.americaslibrary.gov/jp/bball/jp_bball_early_1.html
J	Rap a Tap Tap: Here's Bojangles—Think of That!	Dillon, Leo and Dillon, Diane	Informational Text Picture Book	Social Studies/Arts Culture: Bojangles/Dancer	identify author's purpose	rhymes (Inf./Exp.) letter (Narrative)	contractions words with -ed	rhythm and rhyme; influence of the arts	www.artsedge.kennedy-center.org/interactives/gregoryhines/who/bill-bojangles-robinson
J	What's in Washington, D.C.?	Falk, Laine	Informational Text Picture Book	Social Studies History/USA Heritage	use text features	postcard (Opinion) poster (Inf./Exp.)	pronunciation guides proper nouns	identifying monuments; identifying parts of a city	www.whitehouse.gov/about/inside-white-house/interactive-tour
J	Wild Dogs	Evans, Lynette	Informational Text Picture Book	Science Life Science: Animal Traits and Behaviors	use text features	opinion (Opinion) sidebar (Inf./Exp.)	sound /ou/ words with long a	differentiating between predators and prey; understanding body language	https://www.nwf.org/Kids/Ranger-Rick/Animals/Mammals/Coyotes.aspx
J	Wonderful Worms	Glaser, Linda	Informational Text Picture Book	Science Life Science: Earthworms	ask/answer questions	fact card (Inf./Exp.) words (Inf./Exp.)	adjective words with r-controlled vowels	describing animal motions; identifying elements of a garden	www.urbanext.illinois.edu/worms/
J	Young Cam Jansen and the Lost Tooth	Adler, David A.	Realistic Fiction Picture Book		make predictions	a sign (Inf./Exp.) diary entry (Narrative)	words that imitate sounds words with oo	helping friends; losing baby teeth	http://www.pbskids.org/games/memory.html
K	10 Things I Can Do to Help My World	Walsh, Melanie	Informational Text Picture Book	Science Ecology/Environment	interpret information	opinion (Opinion) description (Inf./Exp.)	context clues	learning responsibility; helping the planet	http://pbskids.org/zoom/activities/action/way04.html
K	Boy Named Boomer, A	Esiason, Boomer	Autobiography Chapter Book	Social Studies Self-Esteem/Goals	identify author's purpose	trading cards (Inf./Exp.) letter (Narrative)	comparative: -er, -est	valuing teamwork and sportsmanship; working hard to succeed	http://www.allstaractivities.com/sports/football/football-terminology.htm http://www.firstbaseesports.com/football_glossary.html
K	Clifford for President	Figueroa, Acton	Fantasy Picture Book		understand plot	campaign poster (Inf./Exp.) speech (Opinion)	contractions	solving problems; understanding positive and negative campaigns	http://www.congressforkids.net/Elections_index.htm
K	Dandelion's Life, A	Himmelman, John	Informational Text Picture Book	Science Life Science/Plant and Animal Life	identify author's purpose	diagram (Inf./Exp.) story (Narrative)	phrases where or when	learning about nature; identifying the stages of a plant's life	http://www.fcps.edu/islandcreekes/ecology/common_dandelion.htm
K	Have You Seen Birds?	Oppenheim, Joanne	Informational Text Picture Book	Science Life Science: Birds	identify main idea and details	sentences (Inf./Exp.) story (Narrative)	rhyming words	identifying the four seasons; understanding descriptive language	http://animals.sandiegozoo.org/content/birds
K	Monarch Butterflies	Alexander, Karen	Informational Text Picture Book	Science Life Science/Butterfly Migration	understand sequence of events	travelog (Narrative) questions/answers (Inf./Exp.)	contractions using 's	learning about monarch butterfly characteristics; discovering why North American monarchs are unique	http://kids.nationalgeographic.com/kids/animals/creaturefeature/monarch-butterflies/
K	Ruby Bridges Goes to School	Bridges, Ruby	Autobiography Photo Essay	Social Studies US History: Civil Rights	connect a series of historical events	write a letter (Opinion) sequence chart (Inf./Exp.)	plurals	recognizing the power of persistence; identifying tolerance and diversity as virtues	http://www.pbs.org/wnet/aaworld/history/spotlight_september.html
K	Sky Color	Reynolds, Peter H.	Realistic Fiction Picture Book		understand problem and solution	draw and label (Inf./Exp.) dialogue (Narrative)	irregular past-tense verbs words with r-controlled vowels	creating art; brainstorming	http://www.peterhreynolds.com/art.html
K	Skyscrapers	York, Vanessa	Informational Text Picture Book	Social Studies Culture/Buildings of the World	understand words and phrases	chart (Inf./Exp.) opinion (Opinion)	proper nouns	learning about the tallest buildings in the world; discovering what skyscrapers are made of	http://www.archkidecture.org/
K	Tree is a Plant, A	Bulla, Clyde Robert	Informational Text Picture Book	Science Life Cycles: Fruit Trees	understand sequence	draw and label (Inf./Exp.) answer a question (Opinion)	consonant blends	exploring how seasons affect plants; learning about the life cycle of fruit trees	http://www.slideshare.net/brockjustine/explain-the-life-cycle-of-a-tree
L	Biblioburro	Winter, Jeanette	Informational Text Picture Book	Social Studies World Cultures: Colombian Community	use information from illustrations and text	make a poster (Inf./Exp.) write/character (Opinion)	homophones	exploring different cultures; knowing the importance of having access to books	http://www.ayokaproductions.org/content/biblioburro-donkey-library

* Titles are CCSS exemplar texts.

Level	Title	Author	Genre/Text Type	Content Area	Comprehension Analyze Text	Writing Options	Phonics/ Word Study	Themes/Ideas	Technology
L	City Tales	Smith, Geof	Realistic Fiction Picture Book		determine meanings of words	T-chart (Narrative) noting character (Narrative)	prefixes contractions	using imagination; finding fun on a rainy day	http://pbskids.org/lions/stories
L	Elephants	Riggs, Kate	Informational Text Picture Book	Science Life Science: Elephants	determine the main idea	chart (Inf./Exp.) fable (Narrative)	three-syllable words comparative endings -er and -est	understanding elephant behavior; learning the location of habitats	www.worldwildlife.org/species/elephant
L	Frogs!	Carney, Elizabeth	Informational Text Chapter Book		compare and contrast	comic scene (Narrative) word web (Inf./Exp.)	words with -ing	describing the life cycle of an animal; recognizing the needs of living organisms	http://animals.sandiegozoo.org/animals/frog-toad
L	House for Hermit Crab, A	Carle, Eric	Fantasy Picture Book		understand problem/ solution	book (Inf./Exp.) dialogue (Narrative)	adverbs ending in -ly	learning about sea creatures; understanding the fear of change	http://library.thinkquest.org/05aug/0106/hermitcrabs.htm
L	Panda Kindergarten	Ryder, Joanne	Informational Text Photo Essay	Social Studies Protecting Wildlife	ask and answer questions	make a poster (Opinion) Venn diagram (Inf./Exp.)	adjectives ending in y	watching young animals grow up; volunteering to help the environment	www.worldwildlife.org/species/giant-panda
L	We Are Alike, We Are Different	Behrens, Janice	Informational Text Picture Book	Social Studies Diversity	understand structure	comparison (Inf./Exp.) word story (Narrative)	plural nouns	realizing the beauty in being different; learning empathy	http://www.cyh.com/HealthTopics/HealthTopicDetailsKids.aspx?p=335&np=286&id=2345
L	What Do Roots Do?	Kudlinski, Kathleen V.	Informational Text Picture Book	Science Life Science: Identifying Plant Parts	identify main idea and details	diagram (Inf./Exp.) letter (Opinion)	synonyms	discovering how trees and plants survive; learning why roots are important	http://urbanext.illinois.edu/gpe/case1/index.html
L	*What Do You Do With a Tail Like This?	Jenkins, Steve and Page, Robin	Informational Text Picture Book	Science Life Science: Animal Traits	determine author's purpose	story (Narrative) fact cards (Inf./Exp.)	words with long i	learning about nature; understanding the diversity of animals	http://www.eduplace.com/kids/hmsc/activities/simulations/gr3/unit8.html
L	Winter Wonderland	Esbaum, Jill	Informational Text Picture Book	Science Earth Science: Seasons/ Winter Weather	identify point of view	poem (Narrative) description (Inf./Exp.)	compound words	appreciating the good things winter brings; understanding winter	http://www.weatherwizkids.com/weather-winter-storms.htm
M	*Bat Loves the Night	Davies, Nicola	Informational Text Picture Book	Science Life Science: Bats	use images and text to show understanding	summary (Narrative) story (Narrative)	compound words	understanding how animals survive; understanding the animal food chain	http://www.bats.org.uk/pages/batsforkids.html
M	Chameleons Are Cool	Jenkins, Martin	Informational Text Picture Book	Science Life Science: Chameleons	identify purpose; point of view	fact cards (Inf./Exp.) description (Inf./Exp.)	adverbs multisyllabic words	learning about unique animals; understanding how animals adapt	www.nwf.org/Kids/Ranger-Rick/Animals/Amphibians-and-Reptiles/Chameleons.aspx
M	Dive! A Book of Deep-Sea Creatures	Berger, Melvin	Informational Text	Science Life Science: Marine Biology	make comparisons	brochure (Opinion) list (Opinion)	words with apostrophes	categorizing animal attributes; understanding deep-sea exploration	www.smithsonianmag.com/science-nature/The-Scariest-Monsters-of-the-Sea-17601371.html
M	Eye for Color, An	Wing, Natasha	Biography Picture Book	Science Art and Science	use visual information	comparison (Inf./Exp.) record (Inf./Exp.)	regular past-tense verbs	teaching others about art; viewing art in a different way	http://www.bbc.co.uk/cbbc/games/colour-factory-game
M	Frida	Winter, Jonah	Biography Picture Book	Social Studies Mexican Culture: Female Artist	connect biographical events	analysis (Inf./Exp.) story (Narrative)	vivid verbs	noting how something good can come from something bad; recognizing creative expression	http://www.ladap.org/online-exhibits/Spanish-colonial-gallery
M	*From Seed to Plant	Gibbons, Gail	Informational Text Picture Book	Science Health: Healthful Food	use context clues	T-chart (Inf./Exp.) journey (Narrative)	compound words	surviving in nature; growing plants and food	http://kidsgrowingstrong.org/PlantParts and http://urbanext.illinois.edu/gpe/case1/c1m1app.html
M	Martin Luther King, Jr. and the March on Washington	Ruffin, Frances E.	Informational Text Picture Book	Social Studies US History	understand historical events	postcard (Narrative) paragraph (Inf./Exp.)	irregular verbs	understanding how people make a difference; learning about famous Americans	http://seattletimes.com/special/mlk/king/timeline.html
M	*Throw Your Tooth on the Roof	Beeler, Selby B.	Informational Text Picture Book	Social Studies World Cultures: Tales	compare and contrast ideas	story (Inf./Exp.) postcard (Opinion)	words with long o spelled ow	exploring childhood traditions; learning world geography	http://kidshealth.org/kid/stay_healthy/body/teeth_care.html
M	Two Bobbies: A True Story of Hurricane Katrina	Larson, Kirby and Nethery, Mary	Informational Text Historical Fiction Picture Book	Social Studies Historical Events: Hurricane Katrina	identify main idea and key details	poster (Inf./Exp.) newspaper (Inf./Exp.)	context clues	celebrating volunteers, helpers, and heroes; recognizing how helping others helps oneself	http://teacher.scholastic.com/activities/wwatch/hurricanes/ready.htm
M	Why Do Dogs Bark?	Holub, Joan	Informational Text Question & Answer Book	Science Life Science: Dog Traits	ask and answer questions	interview (Inf./Exp.) how-to (Inf./Exp.)	suffixes compound words	analyzing animal behavior; understanding responsible pet ownership	http://www.akc.org/breeds/complete_breed_list.cfm
N	Butterfly Boy	Kroll, Virginia	Realistic Fiction Picture Book		identify theme	story (Narrative) trading cards (Inf./Exp.)	verb ending -ed	appreciating the wonders of nature; being open to different ways to communicate	www.butterfliesandmoths.org/species/Vanessa-atalanta
N	Looking Closely in the Rain Forest	Serafini, Frank	Informational Text Picture Book	Science: Biomes Tropical Rain Forests	evaluate author's purpose	riddle (Narrative) review (Opinion)	vivid verbs	using your imagination; finding out how animals adapt	http://animals.sandiegozoo.org/habitats/tropical-rain-forest
N	Magic School Bus Fixes a Bone, The	Earhart, Kristin	Informational Text/ Fantasy Chapter Book	Science Human Body	understand sequence	scene (Narrative) draw and label (Inf./Exp.)	wordplay	identifying body parts; describing what doctors do	http://kidshealth.org/kid/htbw/bones.html
N	My Light	Bang, Molly	Informational Text Picture Book	Science Physical Science: Light	describe relationships between ideas	poster (Inf./Exp.) poem (Narrative)	words with ou and ow	understanding the sun's energy; understanding the connection between nature and electricity	http://www.eia.gov/kids/

* Titles are CCSS exemplar texts.

Level	Title	Author	Genre/Text Type	Content Area	Comprehension Analyze Text	Writing Options	Phonics/ Word Study	Themes/Ideas	Technology
N	Odd Animal Helpers	Reyes, Gabrielle	Informational Text Picture Book	Science Life Science: Symbiotic Relationships	use text features	facts (Inf./Exp.) story (Narrative)	context clues	understanding the concept of partnership; exploring the ways animals meet basic needs	http://www.seaphotos.com/symbiosis.html
N	Owls	Gibbons, Gail	Informational Text Picture Book	Science Life Science: Owls	interpret information	flow chart (Inf./Exp.) opinion (Opinion)	words with long a	learning the importance of saving endangered owls; learning the importance of preserving natural habitats	http://www.nwf.org/kids/family-fun/outdoor-activities/learn-about-owls.aspx
N	Paperboy, The	Pilkey, Dav	Realistic Fiction Picture Book		use illustrations to understand text	question (Narrative) write and draw (Inf./Exp.)	compound words context clues	appreciating the reward of doing a good job; understanding that a person can enjoy being alone	http://sni.scholastic.com/SN3/05_o6_13_SN3/book#/1
N	Pet Heroes	Corse, Nicole	Informational Text Chapter Book	Social Studies Animals Help People	identify main idea and key details	interview (Inf./Exp.) opinion (Opinion)	multisyllabic words	learning that pets can have important jobs; learning the versatility of animals	http://www.fbi.gov/fun-games/kids/kids-dogs
N	Picture Book of Jesse Owens, A	Adler, David A.	Biography Picture Book	Social Studies History: African American Olympic Champion	ask and answer questions	sports card (Inf./Exp.) letter (Opinion)	words with -ed	fighting for equality; making world history	www.jesseowens.com
N	Surprising Swimmers	Ryan, Emma	Informational Text Picture Book	Science Life Science: Animal Behaviors	use text features	poster (Inf./Exp.) explanation (Inf./Exp.)	proper nouns	understanding wild and domestic animals; understanding how animals move	http://animal.discovery.com/mammals/marine-mammals.htm
O	Apples to Oregon	Hopkinson, Deborah	Historical Fiction Picture Book		understand theme	summary (Narrative) list (Inf./Exp)	idioms	inferring character traits; understanding challenges	http://www.oregontrail.com/hmh/site/oregontrail
O	Beachcombing	Arnosky, Jim	Informational Text Picture Book	Science Life Science: Seashore	determine meaning of words	journal entry (Narrative) dialogue (Narrative)	adjectives	identifying ocean species; comparing organism characteristics	http://www.nps.gov/fiis/naturescience/horseshoe-crabs.htm
O	Busy Body Book, The	Rockwell, Lizzy	Informational Text Picture Book	Science Life Science: Human Body	identify main idea and details	poster (Inf./Exp.) summary (Inf./Exp.)	strong verbs commas in a series	exploring physical activities; taking care of your body	http://www.pbs.org/parents/food-and-fitness/sport-and-fitness/motivating-kids-to-get-fit/
O	Coming to America: The Story of Immigration	Maestro, Betsy	Informational Text Picture Book	Social Studies Immigration	describe a series of historical events	story (Narrative) captions (Inf./Exp.)	prefixes relative pronouns	studying US history; learning about immigration	http://www.ellisisland.org/Immexp/index.asp http://www.history.com/topics/united-states-immigration-to-1965
O	In the Garden With Dr. Carver	Grigsby, Susan	Historical Fiction Picture Book		describe characters	poem (Narrative) similes (Narrative)	figurative language	revitalizing a community; learning from others	http://fieldmuseum.org/about/traveling-exhibitions/george-washington-carver
O	Manfish	Berne, Jennifer	Biography Picture Book	Science Marine Biology	summarize text	poem (Narrative) summary (Inf./Exp.)	compound words	understanding our impact on ocean life; taking action to protect oceans	www.cousteau.org
O	Planets	Carney, Elizabeth	Informational Text Picture Book	Science Earth Science: Planets	identify details	facts poster (Opinion) paragraph (Inf./Exp.)	multiple-meaning words	comparing parts of the solar system; recognizing earth's place in space	http://solarsystem.nasa.gov/kids/index.cfm
O	Rocks and Minerals	Zoehfeld, Kathleen Weidner	Informational Text Picture Book	Science Geology	explain how illustrations support text	explanation (Inf./Exp.) description (Narrative)	multisyllabic words	understanding rocks and minerals; learning about rocks and minerals	http://studyjams.scholastic.com/studyjams/jams/science/rocks-minerals-landforms/minerals.htm http://studyjams.scholastic.com/studyjams/jams/science/rocks-minerals-landforms/rock-cycle.htm
O	Sonia Sotomayor: A Judge Grows in the Bronx	Winter, Jonah	Biography Picture Book	Social Studies Latino Woman: Government	determine the meaning of words and phrases	fact cards (Inf./Exp.) questions (Inf./Exp.)	figurative language	learning to have pride in one's background; recognizing that people of all backgrounds should have a voice in government	http://www.timeforkids.com/news/justice-no-other/13361
O	Tell Me, Tree	Gibbons, Gail	Informational Text Picture Book	Science Life Science: Trees	understand cause and effect	review (Opinion) process (Inf./Exp.)	antonyms	identifying steps in a process; understanding the importance of natural resources	http://www.realtrees4kids.org/threefive.htm
P	Amelia and Eleanor Go for a Ride	Ryan, Pam Muñoz	Historical Fiction/ Informational Text Picture Book	Social Studies American History: Famous Women	compare and contrast characters	invitation (Narrative) description (Inf./Exp.)	multisyllabic words	understanding friendship; studying historic figures	http://www.ameliaearhartmuseum.org/AmeliaEarhart/AEFunFacts.htm
P	Boy Who Harnessed the Wind, The	Kamkwamba, William and Mealer, Bryan	Biography Picture Book	Social Studies African Culture: Being a Hero	identify text structure	theme (Inf./Exp.) narrative (Narrative)	regular and irregular past-tense verbs	taking responsibility for others; transforming lives	http://movingwindmills.org/
P	Girl Wonder	Hopkinson, Deborah	Historical Fiction Picture Book		describe characters	journal (Narrative) summary (Narrative)	idioms	learning about women in history; understanding how ideas and beliefs change over time	http://www.exploratorium.edu/baseball/girlsofsummer.html
P	Grandma's Gift	Velasquez, Eric	Realistic Fiction Picture Book	Social Studies	make inferences	skit (Narrative) response (Opinion)	words with apostrophes	discovering identity; understanding the role of culture	http://www.ericvelasquez.com http://www.metmuseum.org/collections/search-the-collections/437869
P	If I Ran for President	Stier, Catherine	Realistic Fiction Picture Book		identify words and phrases	slogan (Inf./Exp.) speech (Opinion)	suffixes	having aspirations; listening to others	http://www.icivics.org/games/win-white-house

* Titles are CCSS exemplar texts.

Level	Title	Author	Genre/Text Type	Content Area	Comprehension Analyze Text	Writing Options	Phonics/Word Study	Themes/Ideas	Technology
P	Life in the Ocean	Nivola, Claire A.	Biography Picture Book	Science Sylvia Earle: Oceanography	explain how illustrations support text	account (Opinion) description (Inf./Exp.)	similes	learning about the earth; learning how people can make a difference	http://www.achievement.org/autodoc/page/ear0bio-1
P	Moon, The	Simon, Seymour	Informational Text Picture Book	Science Earth Science: Moon	recognize cause and effect	T-chart (Inf./Exp.) postcard (Narrative)	context clues	understanding the work astronauts do; identifying the phases of the moon	http://solarsystem.nasa.gov/planets/profile.cfm?Object=Moon
P	* So You Want to Be an Inventor?	St. George, Judith	Informational Text Picture Book	Social Studies Inventors & Inventions	identify supporting reasons and evidence	list (Inf./Exp.) opinion (Opinion)	Greek roots	describing how inventions have changed lives; learning about American and European history	http://web.mit.edu/invent/i-archive.html
P	Take a Giant Leap, Neil Armstrong!	Roop, Peter and Roop, Connie	Biography Chapter Book	Science Earth Science: Young Astronaut	identify text structure	opinion (Opinion) time line (Inf./Exp.)	prefixes	learning about famous people; showing determination	http://www.nasa.gov/centers/glenn/about/bios/neilabio.html
P	Wolverine vs. Tasmanian Devil	Pallotta, Jerry	Informational Text Magazine Format	Science Life Science: Predator Traits	compare and contrast	ending (Narrative) comparison (Opinion)	suffixes: -ous, -full, -less double medial consonants	defining a rivalry; analyzing advantages	http://animal.discovery.com/mammals/marsupials.htm
Q	Amazing Magnetism	Carmi, Rebecca	Informational Text/ Fantasy Chapter Book	Science: Physical Science Magnetism	analyze story structure	riddle (Inf./Exp.) evaluation (Opinion)	multiple-meaning words	thinking creatively; solving problems	http://www.scholastic.com/play/junk.htm
Q	Away West	McKissick, Patricia	Historical Fiction Chapter Book		determine the theme	rewrite (Narrative) description (Inf./Exp.)	compound words	learning about the experiences of African Americans; setting goals	http://www.nps.gov/nico/index.htm
Q	Barnum's Bones	Fern, Tracey	Biography Picture Book	Science Archeology: Scientist Discovers T-Rex Bones	determine meaning of words	placard (Inf./Exp.) letter (Narrative)	affixes and roots	pursuing a passion or a dream; learning about paleontology	http://www.amnh.org/explore/news-blogs/news-posts/npr-traces-history-of-barnum-brown-s-first-t-rex-skeleton
Q	Bugs	Arlon, Penelope and Gordon-Harris, Tory	Informational Text Picture Book	Science Life Science: Bug Traits	interpret text and visuals	diagram (Inf./Exp.) dialogue (Narrative)	context clues	using charts and graphs; asking and answering questions	www.scholastic.com/discovermore
Q	Camping Trip That Changed America, The	Rosenstock, Barb	Informational Text Picture Book	Social Studies History: National Parks	recognize sequence	conversation (Narrative) letter (Opinion)	compound words	exploring nature; taking a trip	http://www.sierraclub.org/john_muir_exhibit/life/in_yosemite_by_roosevelt.aspx
Q	Dinosaurs	Arlon, Penelope and Gordon-Harris, Tory	Informational Text Magazine Format	Science Life Science: Traits of Dinosaurs	summarize text	poster (Inf./Exp.) fact chart (Inf./Exp.)	context clues	understanding science concepts; using illustrations	www.scholastic.com/discovermore
Q	* Medieval Feast, A	Aliki	Informational Text Picture Book	Social Studies Medieval History	identify key details in text and art	invitation (Inf./Exp.) thank you (Narrative)	context clues	recognizing where food comes from; learning about different cultures	http://www.childrensmuseum.org/castles/games.php
Q	Playing to Win	Deans, Karen	Biography Picture Book	Social Studies African American Women/Sports	identify main idea and supporting details	letter (Inf./Exp.) list (Opinion)	suffixes	understanding the value of perseverance; identifying important achievements	http://www.altheagibson.com
Q	Testing the Ice	Robinson, Sharon	Biography Picture Book	Social Studies Family/Fathers Fight Racism	draw inferences	letter (Narrative) poster (Inf./Exp.)	commas spelling changes with suffixes	fighting racial barriers; appreciating family closeness	www.history.com/topics/jackie-robinson
Q	WordGirl: Tobey or Consequences	Various	Comedy/Fantasy Teleplay		describe characters	scene (Narrative) story (Narrative)	formal vs. informal language	recognizing good vs. evil; learning about the production of an animated series	http://pbskids.org/wordgirl
R	Annie Sullivan and the Trials of Helen Keller	Lambert, Joseph	Biography Graphic Novel	Social Studies Heroes: Overcoming Challenges	integrate information from illustrations	narrative (Narrative) time line (Inf./Exp.)	onomatopoeia	understanding a person's achievements; recognizing how individuals set and reach goals	www.afb.org/section.aspx?PolderID=1&SectionID=1&TopicID=194
R	Buzz on Bees, The	Rotner, Shelley and Woodhull, Anne	Informational Text Photo Essay	Science Earth/Life Science: Vanishing Honeybees	analyze text structure	chart (Inf./Exp.) mystery (Narrative)	context clues	understanding pollination; identifying ways to help save bees	http://kids.discovery.com/tell-me/animals/bug-world/bee-world
R	Everything Dolphin	Crisp, Marty	Informational Text Picture Book	Science Life Science: Dolphin Traits	explain author's use of evidence	poster (Inf./Exp.) opinion (Opinion)	context clues	learning about an animal's unique features and abilities; finding answers to questions	http://video.pbs.org/video/1778560486/
R	* Horses	Simon, Seymour	Informational Text Picture Book	Social Studies/Science Horse Traits/Helping People	summarize text	description (Narrative) summary (Inf./Exp.)	suffix -ly	learning about living things; recognizing species diversity	http://horsebreedsinfo.com/
R	Looking Like Me	Myers, Walter Dean	Realistic Fiction Picture Book		identify structural elements	comparison (Inf./Exp.) description (Narrative)	formal vs. informal language	celebrating traits/abilities of others; recognizing that each person is unique	http://www.walterdeanmyers.net/index.html http://www.scholastic.com/teachers/contributor/christopher-myers
R	Luis Alvarez: Wild Idea Man	Venezia, Mike	Biography Picture Book	Science Spanish American Inventor	draw inferences	questions (Inf./Exp.) opinion (Opinion)	suffixes	understanding the value of curiosity; participating in science for the sake of science	http://newscenter.lbl.gov/feature-stories/2010/03/09/alvarez-theory-on-dinosaur/

* Titles are CCSS exemplar texts.

Level	Title	Author	Genre/Text Type	Content Area	Comprehension Analyze Text	Writing Options	Phonics/Word Study	Themes/Ideas	Technology
R	Queen of the Track	Lang, Heather	Biography Picture Book	Social Studies Culture: African American Female Athlete Faces Challenges	make inferences	journal entry (Narrative) profile (Inf./Exp.)	figurative language	understanding prejudice and racial discrimination; identifying the qualities of Olympic athletes	http://heatherlangbooks.com/Queen-Of-The-Track.html
R	Sadako and the Thousand Paper Cranes	Coerr, Eleanor	Historical Fiction Chapter Book		analyze characters	letter (Inf./Exp.) review (Opinion)	compound words	understanding beliefs and traditions; transforming tragedy into hope	http://web-japan.org/kidsweb/virtual/index.html
R	Trail of Tears, The	Bruchac, Joseph	Informational Text Chapter Book	Social Studies History: Relocating Cherokee	analyze events in historical text	character study (Opinion) time line (Inf./Exp.)	prefix dis-	making a difficult journey; fighting for your rights	http://www.gpb.org/georgiastories/videos/trail_of_tears
R	*Volcanoes	Simon, Seymour	Informational Text Chapter Book	Science: Earth Science Volcanoes	explain concepts in a scientific text	poster (Inf./Exp.) description (Narrative)	multisyllabic words	explaining scientific concepts; comparing and contrasting	http://www.nps.gov/havo/photosmultimedia/lava-flows-hotspots.htm
S	Cod's Tale, The	Kurlansky, Mark	Informational Text Picture Book	Social Studies Culture: Cod's Impact on the World	use text features	poster (Inf./Exp.) time line (Inf./Exp.)	comparative adjectives	learning about world history; understanding food chains	http://www.arkive.org/atlantic-cod/gadus-morhua/
S	Dancing Home	Ada, Alma Flor	Realistic Fiction Chapter Book		compare and contrast characters	Venn diagram (Inf./Exp.) letter (Narrative)	foreign words	moving to a new country; exploring what it means to be American	http://almaflorada.com/dancing-home
S	Helen Keller: Her Life in Pictures	Sullivan, George	Biography Photo Essay	Social Studies Famous Women: Overcoming Challenges	integrating information	summary (Inf./Exp.) email (Inf./Exp.)	vivid verbs	recognizing women who made a difference; recognizing how individuals set and reach goals	http://pbskids.org/arthur/print/braille/braille_guide.html
S	Lizards	Bishop, Nic	Informational Text Picture Book	Science Life Science: Lizards: Adaptation/Traits	interpret visual information	favorite (Opinion) flashcards (Inf./Exp.)	figurative language	adapting to an environment; learning about interesting animals	http://animals.sandiegozoo.org/animals/lizard
S	Louie: The Stray Who Was Saved	Rense, Paige	Informational Text/ Fantasy Picture Book	Social Studies People Caring for Stray Animals	understand point of view	description (Inf./Exp.) essay (Opinion)	changing verbs to nouns long a spelled ay, ei, a	demonstrating compassion; appreciating art	http://www.artnet.com/artists/kenneth-noland/
S	Martin's Big Words	Rappaport, Doreen	Biography Picture Book	Social Studies History: Civil Rights Leader	determine main ideas and explain details	poem (Narrative) opinion (Opinion)	antonyms	learning about tolerance and acceptance; learning about the civil rights movement	http://www.nobelprize.org/nobel_prizes/peace/laureates/1964/king-bio.html
S	Monster Hunt	Arnosky, Jim	Informational Text Picture Book	Science Life Science/Phenomena: Cryptology	summarize information	log (Narrative) plaque (Inf./Exp.)	scientific names	solving mysteries; finding scientific explanations	www.newanimal.org
S	Nelson Mandela	Nelson, Kadir	Biography Picture Book	Social Studies World Leaders: Overcoming Challenges	use context clues	scene (Narrative) opinion (Opinion)	figurative language	recognizing great leaders; fighting for human rights	http://www.nelsonmandela.org/
S	Neo Leo: The Ageless Ideas of Leonardo da Vinci	Barretta, Gene	Informational Text Picture Book	Science Science and Technology	identify points, reasons, and evidence	speech (Inf./Exp.) story (Narrative)	Latin roots	exploring da Vinci's scientific ideas; connecting modern machines with historic ideas	http://legacy.mos.org/leonardo/
S	Thousand Cranes, A	Miller, Kathryn Schultz	Historical Fiction Play		visualize	diary entry (Narrative) sign (Inf./Exp.)	similes and metaphors	honoring ancestors; coping with death	http://hibakushastories.org/
T	Bad News for Outlaws	Nelson, Vaunda Micheaux	Biography Picture Book	Social Studies African American US Marshall/Old West	explain relationship of events	opinion (Opinion) poster (Inf./Exp.)	suffix -ly	identifying qualities of a hero; learning what it means to be fearless	http://www.usmarshals.gov/usmsforkids/index.html
T	Bill the Boy Wonder	Nobleman, Marc Tyler	Biography Picture Book	Arts Cocreator of Batman	analyze how authors support their points	tribute (Inf./Exp.) defense (Opinion)	figurative language	acknowledging people's accomplishments; learning about the lives of real people	http://www.readwritethink.org/parent-afterschool-resources/games-tools/comic-creator-a-30237.html
T	Great Serum Race, The	Miller, Debbie S.	Informational Text Picture Book	Social Studies History: Teamwork	explain relationships between events	article (Inf./Exp.) journal (Opinion)	multiple-meaning words	working as a team; refusing to give up	http://iditarod.com/
T	Hands Around the Library	Roth, Susan L. and Abouraya, Karen Leggett	Informational Text Picture Book	Social Studies Culture: Egypt's Libraries	identify supporting reasons/evidence	letter (Narrative) opinion (Opinion)	pronouns	creating change; taking a risk to achieve something	http://www.scholastic.com/browse/article.jsp?id=3755645
T	Ida B. Wells: Let the Truth Be Told	Myers, Walter Dean	Biography Picture Book	Social Studies African American Women: Fighting Injustice	make inferences	script (Narrative) summary (Opinion)	prepositions	using words to fight injustice; understanding the contributions of African American women	http://www.biography.com/people/ida-b-wells-9527635
T	Jackie Robinson: American Hero	Robinson, Sharon	Biography Informational Text	Social Studies African American History: Racism in Baseball	quote accurately to support analysis	letter (Narrative) essay (Opinion)	idioms	overcoming prejudice and racial discrimination; identifying the traits of American heroes	http://www.jackierobinson.com/
T	Looking at Lincoln	Kalman, Maira	Biography Picture Book	Social Studies History: Learning About Lincoln	analyze point of view	captions (Inf./Exp.) article (Inf./Exp.)	context clues	identifying background events of importance; realizing that great people live forever	http://www.whitehouse.gov/about/presidents/abrahamlincoln

* Titles are CCSS exemplar texts.

GUIDED READING Nonfiction Focus 2nd Edition

Level	Title	Author	Genre/Text Type	Content Area	Comprehension Analyze Text	Writing Options	Phonics/ Word Study	Themes/Ideas	Technology
T	Muscles	Simon, Seymour	Informational Text Photo Essay	Science Human Body/Muscles	determine meaning	glossary (Inf./Exp.) descriptions (Inf./Exp.)	Latin roots	learning how to keep the body healthy; understanding body structure	http://kidshealth.org/kid/htbw/
T	* My Librarian Is a Camel	Ruurs, Margriet	Informational Text Picture Book	Social Studies Culture: How Books Get to Remote Places	summarize text	story (Narrative) summary (Inf./Exp.)	multiple-meaning words	learning about other countries; understanding how dedicated librarians help children have access to books	http://travelinglibraries.webs.com/aroundtheworld.htm
T	Strongest Man in the World, The	Debon, Nicolas	Historical Fiction Graphic Novel		interpret visual information	article (Inf./Exp.) poster (Opinion)	words in other languages	understanding the importance of family; knowing when to step down	http://www.pbs.org/opb/circus/in-the-ring/history-circus/
U	Abe's Honest Words	Rappaport, Doreen	Informational Text Picture Book	Social Studies American History: Lincoln	identify reasons and evidence	letter (Opinion) description (Inf./Exp.)	Latin roots	opposing injustice and slavery; leading others with dignity	http://www.abrahamlincolnonline.org/lincoln/speeches/quotes.htm http://www.notable-quotes.com/l/lincoln_abraham.html
U	Around the World	Phelan, Matt	Historical Fiction Graphic Novel		use picture details	travel poster (Inf./Exp.) journal (Narrative)	context clues proper nouns	exploring the world; displaying courage	www.expedia.com
U	Boys Who Rocked the World	McCann, Michelle Roehm	Informational Text Chapter Book	Social Studies Profiles of Great Men in Various Fields	read closely to analyze	express an idea (Narrative) Venn diagram (Inf./Exp.)	suffix -ist	recognizing the power of passion and hard work; understanding the importance of trusting one's inner voice	http://www.scholastic.com/browse/article.jsp?id=3756952
U	Fearless	Woodruff, Elvira	Historical Fiction Novel		make inferences	evaluation (Inf./Exp.) position (Opinion)	prefixes	overcoming obstacles; taking care of others	www.england.pharology.eu/Eddystone1698.html
U	Ghost Hunt	Hawes, Jason and Wilson, Grant, with Dokey, Cameron	Science Fiction Short Stories	Science Investigating Science Mysteries	make inferences	checklist (Inf./Exp.) story (Narrative)	adverbs and adjectives	drawing conclusions; coping with fear	http://www.americanfolklore.net/campfire.html
U	I Dreamed of Flying Like a Bird	Haas, Robert B.	Informational Text Photo Essay	Arts Aerial (Animal) Photography	identify details and examples	letter (Opinion) poster (Inf./Exp.)	suffix -ful	seeing the beauty of nature; learning about wild animals in their habitats	http://www.nature.org/photosmultimedia/ markgodfreyselects/mark-godfrey-selects-cameron-davidson.xml
U	Life of Rice, The	Sobol, Richard	Informational Text Photo Essay	Social Studies Food/Culture	explain stated and inferred information	time line (Inf./Exp.) picture essay (Inf./Exp.)	words with suffixes	seeing things through a camera's eye; helping others	http://www.fao.org/docrep/u8480e/u8480e07.htm
U	Titanic Sinks!	Denenberg, Barry	Informational Text Historical Fiction	Social Studies Historical Disaster	understand point of view	answer a question (Inf./Exp.) T-chart (Opinion)	suffixes	recognizing the need to establish correct priorities; understanding the importance of attention to details	http://www.immersionlearning.org
U	Touch the Sky	Irving, Barrington and Peppe, Holly	Autobiography Chapter Book	Social Studies African American/Pilot	explain the relationship of events	letter (Inf./Exp.) opinion (Opinion)	difficult words	learning about key events in a real person's life; overcoming challenges	http://www.experienceaviation.org/
U	Wright Brothers' First Flight, The	de Lancie, John and Segaloff, Nat	Biography Radio Play	Science Inventions/Aviation	understand structural elements/drama	journal entry (Narrative) time line (Inf./Exp.)	colloquialisms and idioms	working together; innovating	http://airandspace.si.edu/exhibitions/wright-brothers/online/
V	Dear America: So Far From Home	Binder, Carl	Drama/Historical Fiction Teleplay		understand cause and effect	episode (Narrative) speech (Inf./Exp.)	colloquial language	overcoming obstacles; understanding American history	www.historyplace.com/unitedstates/childlabor
V	Detector Dogs: Canines That Save Lives	Stamper, Judith Bauer	Informational Text Magazine Format	Social Studies Canine Heroes	determine main ideas and key details	letter to editor (Opinion) story (Narrative)	suffixes -or and -er	understanding friendship; valuing dogs as more than pets	http://video.pbs.org/video/1475527358
V	Emperor's Silent Army, The	O'Connor, Jane	Informational Text Chapter Book	Social Studies Ancient Chinese History: Culture	determine meaning of words in context	brochure (Opinion) report (Inf./Exp.)	prefixes	understanding an ancient culture; recognizing the value of archaeology	http://whc.unesco.org/en/list/441/video
V	Ice! The Amazing History of the Ice Business	Pringle, Laurence	Informational Text Picture Book	Social Studies History/Inventions	explain the relationships between events	letter (Narrative) book review (Opinion)	negative prefixes	understanding how progress changed America; appreciating history	http://www.greatachievements.org/default.aspx?id=2984
V	Into the Volcano	O'Meara, Donna	Informational Text Magazine Format	Science Earth Science/Scientist: Volcanoes	interpret/integrate information	newspaper report (Narrative) diagram (Inf./Exp.)	understanding roots	learning about scientific work; recognizing women's contributions to science	http://www.scholastic.com/play/prevolcano.htm
V	King George: What Was His Problem?	Sheinkin, Steve	Informational Text Chapter Book	Social Studies History: Cause/Effect of American Revolution	understand cause and effect	causal chain (Inf./Exp.) profile (Narrative)	base words	supporting an opinion; interpreting figurative language	http://www.socialstudiesforkids.com/subjects/revolutionarywar.htm
V	My Havana	Wells, Rosemary	Memoir Chapter Book	Social Studies Culture: Moving to New Countries	make inferences	letter (Narrative) Venn diagram (Inf./Exp.)	foreign words	coping with homesickness; learning about other countries	www.loc.gov/pictures/search/?q=havana%20cuba&gr=true
V	Rebel in a Dress: Adventurers	Branzei, Sylvia	Biography Chapter Book	Social Studies History: Remarkable Women	identify main idea and key details	letter (Narrative) opinion (Opinion)	context clues	learning about the lives of real people; exploring what it means to be a rebel and an adventurer	http://www.worldrecordacademy.com/travel/longest_journey_around_the_world-world_record_set_by_Rosie_Swale_Pope_80263.htm

* Titles are CCSS exemplar texts.

Level	Title	Author	Genre/Text Type	Content Area	Comprehension Analyze Text	Writing Options	Phonics/ Word Study	Themes/Ideas	Technology
V	Thunder From the Sea	Weigel, Jeff	Historical Fiction Graphic Novel		analyze characters' responses to events	recommendation (Opinion) time line (Inf./Exp.)	dialect	learning what's right and wrong; caring about others	http://www.nps.gov/sama/forkids/upload/PartsShip.pdf
V	Unexpected World of Nature, The	Various	Informational Text/ Fantasy Graphic Novel	Science Life Science: Animals in Danger	explain stated and inferred information	journal (Narrative) list (Inf./Exp.)	nouns with the suffix -ology	understanding the importance of saving habits; comparing fact with fantasy	http://www.pbs.org/wnet/nature/lessons/conservation-nation/video-segments-the-wolf-thatchanged-america/4858/
W	At Ellis Island: A History in Many Voices	Peacock, Louise	Informational Text Picture Book	Social Studies: History First-Person Accounts of Ellis Island	analyze point of view	letter (Narrative) summary (Inf./Exp.)	suffixes -tion, -ation	understanding the importance of family; taking a chance	www.nps.gov/elis/index.htm
W	Baby Mammoth Mummy Frozen in Time!	Sloan, Christopher	Informational Text Magazine Format	Science Scientists/Prehistoric Animals	analyze main idea/details	brochure (Inf./Exp.) myth (Narrative)	using word parts	understanding the jobs of scientists; finding clues to prehistoric life	http://www.bbc.co.uk/nature/life/Woolly_mammoth
W	Down to the Last Out	Myers, Walter Dean	Informational Text Novel		analyze point of view	comic strip (Narrative) sketch (Inf./Exp.)	context clues	playing with good sportsmanship; acting with dignity	www.nlbm.com http://mlb.mlb.com/mlb/history/mlb_negro_leagues.jsp
W	Drawing From Memory	Say, Allen	Memoir Picture Book	Arts/Culture Discovering Talents/ Honoring One's Roots	explain relationship of events	account (Narrative) list (Inf./Exp.)	prefixes and suffixes	accepting guidance; finding creative inspiration	www.rif.org/kids/readingplanet/bookzone/say.htm
W	Freedom Heroines	Wishinsky, Frieda	Biography Chapter Book	Social Studies Famous Women: Women's Rights	analyze cause and effect	editorial (Opinion) analysis (Inf./Exp.)	suffixes -er and -or	learning about women in American history; recognizing an individual's contributions to society	http://www.winningthevote.org/
W	Kubla Khan: The Emperor of Everything	Krull, Kathleen	Informational Text Picture Book	Social Studies World Leaders	identify main idea and details	letter (Opinion) question/answer (Inf./Exp.)	suffixes -ion, -tion	understanding what makes a leader; learning about a different time and place	http://www.history.com/topics/kublai-khan
W	Tornado!	Fradin, Judith Bloom and Fradin, Dennis Brindell	Informational Text Magazine Format	Science Meteorology/Tornadoes	analyze multiple accounts of an event	story (Narrative) poster (Inf./Exp.)	Greek and Latin roots	understanding the destructive nature of tornadoes; reading first-person accounts about surviving a tornado	http://www.ready.gov/tornadoes
W	Walt Whitman: Words for America	Kerley, Barbara	Biography Picture Book	Social Studies/Arts Writer's Response to the Civil War	analyze information between texts	interview (Inf./Exp.) ad (Opinion)	word choice	noting how art reflects society; learning how poets express themselves	http://www.poetryarchive.org/childrensarchive/home.do
W	Who Wants Pizza?	Thornhill, Jan	Informational Text Magazine Format	Science Analyzing Food/Nutrition	understand and evaluate arguments	summary (Inf./Exp.) editorial (Opinion)	multisyllabic words	learning the history of food; identifying ecological problems	http://www.chooseemyplate.gov/food-groups/
W	Wonderstruck	Selznick, Brian	Historical Fiction Graphic Novel		compare visual elements with text	description (Opinion) letter (Opinion)	multisyllabic words	connecting with others; influencing other lives	www.amnh.org/explore
X	Alexander Hamilton: The Outsider	Fritz, Jean	Biography Chapter Book	Social Studies Alexander Hamilton: Success Story	determine author's point of view	time line (Inf./Exp.) captions (Inf./Exp.)	affixes	understanding our country's founding; the roots of American politics and economics	www.alexanderhamiltonexhibition.org
X	Black Hole Is Not a Hole, A	Decristofano, Carolyn Cinami	Informational Text/ Mysteries Magazine Format	Science Discoveries of Black Holes	categorize information	visual (Inf./Exp.) book review (Opinion)	compound adjectives	understanding physics; identifying scientific advances	http://www.nasa.gov/audience/forstudents/5-8/index.html
X	Case Closed?	Hughes, Susan	Informational Text Chapter Book	Science Using Science to Solve Mysteries	explain relationship of ideas	letter (Narrative) summary (Inf./Exp.)	suffixes -ology, -ologist	learning about ancient peoples; connecting ideas to draw conclusions	http://www.history.com/interactives/myth-vs-reality-exploring-mysteries-of-the-world
X	Fort Mose	Turner, Glennette Tilley	Informational Text Chapter Book	Social Studies History: First Black Settlement in Colonial America	make inferences	story (Narrative) position (Argument)	prefixes	understanding courage; celebrating the achievements of others	www.floridastateparks.org/fortmose http://www.fortmose.org
X	Great Depression, The	McDaniel, Melissa	Informational Text Chapter Book	Social Studies History: The Great Depression	understand cause and effect	article (Inf./Exp.) essay (Argument)	suffixes -ion, -tion	finding solutions to political problems; understanding experiences of people during the Great Depression	http://www.english.illinois.edu/maps/depression/photoessay.htm
X	Hidden Girl, The	Kaufman, Lola Rein with Metzger, Lois	Autobiography Chapter Book	Social Studies World History: Surviving the Holocaust	analyze how text contributes to ideas	letter (Argument) news article (Inf./Exp.)	figurative language	studying photography; studying politics	http://www.ushmm.org/exhibition/silent-witness/
X	Lincoln Through the Lens	Sandler, Martin W.	Biography Photo Essay	Social Studies History/Photographs and Text Tell Lincoln's Story	make inferences based on the main idea	speech (Opinion) sketch (Inf./Exp.)	multisyllabic words	changing people's opinions; doing what is right	http://rogerjnorton.com/Lincoln2.html
X	Lions of Little Rock, The	Levine, Kristin	Historical Fiction Novel		analyze characters' actions and motives	letter (Narrative) rebuttal (Argument)	similes/metaphors	overcoming adversity; showing bravery	http://www.pbs.org/wnet/aaworld/timeline/civil_01.html
X	Odyssey of Flight 33,	Serling, Rod	Science Fiction Graphic Novel		determine word meanings and tones	story (Narrative) opinion (Argument)	nonstandard English	recognizing that important decisions require good judgment; recognizing the importance of taking responsibilities seriously	http://www.npr.org/programs/morning/features/patc/twilightzone

* Titles are CCSS exemplar texts.

Level	Title	Author	Genre/Text Type	Content Area	Comprehension Analyze Text	Writing Options	Phonics/Word Study	Themes/Ideas	Technology
X	UFOs: What Scientists Say May Shock You!	Grace, N. B.	Informational Text Magazine Format	Social Studies UFOs: Sightings and Stories	draw conclusions	essay (Argument) story (Narrative)	denotation/connotation	learning about extraterrestrial communication; drawing conclusions about UFO sightings	http://www.space.com/search-for-life/
Y	10 Days: Abraham Lincoln	Colbert, David	Biography Chapter Book	Social Studies US History/10 Days of Lincoln's Life	explain the relationship of events	summary (Inf./Exp.) opinion (Argument)	words with prefixes im- and in-	abolishing slavery; serving the country	http://www.nps.gov/history/logcabin/html/al.html
Y	Assassin	Myers, Anna	Historical Fiction Novel		analyze point of view	retell story (Narrative) news article (Inf./Exp.)	suffix -ist	understanding different perspectives; realizing that good people can make bad decisions	http://www.americaslibrary.gov/jb/civil/jb_civil_lincoln_1.html
Y	Courage Has No Color	Stone, Tanya Lee	Informational Text Chapter/Photo Book	Social Studies US/African American History: First Black Paratroopers	analyze the development of ideas	journal entry (Narrative) summary (Inf./Exp.)	denotation and connotation	analyzing America's race relations; understanding key events in history	www.triplenickle.com
Y	Everything Ancient Egypt	Boyer, Crispin	Informational Text Magazine Format	Social Studies History: Ancient Egypt	identify main idea and key details	report (Inf./Exp.) T-chart (Inf./Exp.)	prefix un-	comparing past and present; recognizing that ideas and beliefs change over time	http://www.ancientegypt.co.uk/menu.html
Y	Gettysburg	Butzer, C. M.	Informational Text Graphic Novel	Social Studies Battle of Gettysburg/Gettysburg Address	analyze illustrations	news story (Inf./Exp.) paraphrase (Inf./Exp.)	unfamiliar words	sacrifice; patriotism	www.civilwar.org/battlefields/gettysburg.html
Y	How They Croaked	Bragg, Georgia	Biography Chapter Book	Social Studies Famous People: Lives and Deaths	understand biography	obituary (Narrative) facts (Inf./Exp.)	idioms	facing mortality; finding connections in history	www.historyorb.com/today/deaths.php
Y	Our Town	Wilder, Thornton	Drama Play		understand how a plot unfolds	descriptions (Inf./Exp.) review (Argument)	dialect	appreciating family; observing life in the past	http://www.pbs.org/wgbh/masterpiece/americancollection/ourtown/ttof_sentinel_qt.html
Y	We've Got a Job: The 1963 Birmingham Children's March	Levinson, Cynthia Y.	Informational Text Chapter Book	Social Studies US History: Civil Rights	determine meaning of words	journal entry (Narrative) letter (Inf./Exp.)	suffixes -ion, -tion, -ation	reading firsthand accounts; standing up for your beliefs	http://www.pbslearningmedia.org/resource/iml04.soc.ush.civil.ahendric/audrey-hendricks/
Y	Whatever Happened to the World of Tomorrow?	Fies, Brian	Historical Fiction/Memoir Graphic Novel	Social Studies Family/Technology	analyze point of view	time line (Inf./Exp.) comic strip (Narrative)	synonyms/antonyms	hoping for a positive future; feeling loyalty and pride toward a person's country	http://www.pbs.org/wgbh/amex/moon/timeline/
Y	World War II	Rosenberg, Aaron	Informational Text Chapter Book	Social Studies World History: World War II Key Figures	understand cause and effect	answer questions (Opinion) time line (Inf./Exp.)	root words	understanding leadership; identifying historical events	www.memory.loc.gov/ammem/collections/maps/wwii/
Z	Ancient Rome	Benoit, Peter	Informational Text Magazine Format	Social Studies History: Ancient Rome	analyze structure and development of ideas	letter (Narrative) report (Inf./Exp.)	possessives	comparing an ancient civilization with our own; understanding how historical events influence people's lives	http://www.bbc.co.uk/ahistoryoftheworld/explorerallflash/?tag=48&tagname=Ancient%20Rome&page=2#topofpage
Z	Catching Fire	Collins, Suzanne	Science Fiction Novel		understand point of view	editorial (Argument) map (Inf./Exp.)	figurative language	falling in love; displaying leadership	www.scholastic.com/thehungergames/index.htm
Z	Dark Game, The	Janeczko, Paul B.	Informational Text Chapter Book	Social Studies Historical Events and Connections	make inferences	journal entry (Narrative) opinion (Argument)	connotation/denotation	learning about people in history; understanding cause and effect	www.nsa.gov/kids/home.shtml
Z	Ghosts in the Fog	Seiple, Samantha	Informational Text Chapter Book	Social Studies History: Japan Invasion World War II	determine author's purpose	time line (Inf./Exp.) journal entry (Narrative)	prefixes	learning about the events of World War II; comparing and contrasting different cultures	www.nps.gov/aleu/index.htm
Z	Joseph Stalin	McCollum, Sean	Biography Chapter Book	Social Studies History: Soviet Dictator	analyze biography	journal entry (Narrative) poster (Argument)	synonyms	exploring a real person's life; identifying traits of a leader	http://www.worldwarii.org/p/comrades-men-and-women-compatriots.html
Z	Monsters Are Due on Maple Street, The	Kneece, Mark	Science Fiction Graphic Novel		understand theme	argument (Argument) script (Narrative)	context clues	living in a community; studying philosophy	http://www.hulu.com/watch/440892
Z	Mysterious Messages	Blackwood, Gary	Informational Text Chapter Book	Social Studies History: Spies & Secret Codes	analyze cause and effect	connection (Inf./Exp.) play (Narrative)	root words	learning about historical events; finding solutions to problems	http://www.spymuseum.org/exhibition-experiences/
Z	Teens at War	Zullo, Allan	Informational Text Chapter Book	Social Studies History: Courage in War	understand characters	letter (Narrative) research (Inf./Exp.)	unfamiliar words	contributing to an effort; showing patriotism	www.loc.gov/pictures/ www.loc.gov/pictures/collection/drwg/
Z	Thoreau at Walden	Porcellino, John	Biography Graphic Novel	Social Studies Writer Thoreau's Unique Journey	analyze point of view/ purpose	opinion (Argument) graphic page (Narrative)	metaphors	placing blame; coping with the unexplained	www.walden.org
Z	Unraveling Freedom	Bausum, Ann	Informational Text Photo/Chapter Book	Social Studies US History/World War II	main idea and details	opinion (Argument) letter (Inf./Exp.)	analyzing multisyllabic words	learning about US history; understanding historical events	http://www.pbs.org/greatwar/timeline/index.html

* Titles are CCSS exemplar texts.

GUIDED READING RESEARCH BASE

Essential Element	Key Ideas—National Reading Panel
Phonemic Awareness Instruction in Guided Reading • Children use their beginning connections between letters and sounds to check on their reading. They notice mismatches. They use letter-sound information to know how words begin. • Teachers prompt children to make their reading "look right."	"Phonemic awareness instruction is not a complete reading program; it cannot guarantee the reading and writing success of your students. Long lasting effects depend on the effectiveness of the whole curriculum." (3, p. 9) "Phonemic awareness instruction does not need to consume long periods of time to be effective. In these analyses, programs lasting less than 20 hours were more effective than longer programs." (2, pp. 2–6) "In addition to teaching phonemic awareness skills with letters, it is important for teachers to help children make the connection between the skills taught and their application to reading and writing tasks." (2, pp. 2–33)
Phonics Instruction in Guided Reading • Teachers select texts that, along with high-frequency words that are available to students, offer opportunities to use phonics skills. • As they introduce texts, support reading, and revisit the text after reading, teachers bring students' attention to features of words and strategies for decoding words. • Students apply word-solving strategies to reading continuous texts. • Teachers explicitly demonstrate how to take words apart and apply phonics principles to new words students meet in continuous text. • Teachers explicitly teach phonics principles through word work after the text is read. Word work sessions are connected to a phonics continuum. • Teachers prompt students to use phonics skills to take words apart while reading.	"Children need opportunities to use what they have learned in problem solving unfamiliar words that they encounter within continuous text. They use word-solving strategies to take words apart while keeping the meaning in mind." (3, p. 18) "Reading words accurately and automatically enables children to focus on the meaning of text." (3) "Programs should acknowledge that systematic phonics instruction is a means to an end. Some phonics programs focus primarily on teaching children a large number of letter-sound relationships. These programs often do not allot enough instructional time to help children learn how to put this knowledge to use in reading actual words, sentences, and texts. Although children need to be taught the major consonant and vowel letter-sound relationships, they also need ample reading and writing activities that allow them to practice this knowledge." (3, p. 17)
Fluency Instruction in Guided Reading • Texts are selected to be within students' control so that they know most of the words and can read fluently (with teaching). • The teacher introduces the text to support comprehension and connections to language. • Teachers draw students' attention to elements of words that will help them recognize or solve them rapidly.	"If text is read in a laborious and inefficient manner, it will be difficult for the child to remember what has been read and to relate the ideas expressed in the text to his or her background knowledge." (1, p. 22) "Repeated and monitored oral reading improves reading fluency and overall reading achievement." (3, p. 11) "It is important to provide students with instruction and practice in fluency as they read connected text." (3, p. 23) "Word recognition is a necessary but not sufficient condition for fluent reading." (3, p. 30) "Fluency is not a stage of development at which readers can read all words quickly and easily. Fluency changes, depending on what readers are reading, their familiarity with the words, and the amount of their practice with reading text." (3, p. 23)

• Teachers help students to understand and use the language patterns that may be found in written text. • Students use word recognition and comprehending strategies in an orchestrated way while reading or rereading a text silently or orally. • Teachers provide explicit demonstrations and instruction in reading fluency. • Teachers prompt for fluency when students are reading aloud. • Students engage in repeated oral readings to work for fluency.	"By listening to good models of fluent reading, students learn how a reader's voice can help written text make sense." (3, p. 26) "Fluency develops as a result of many opportunities to practice reading with a high degree of success. Therefore, your students should practice orally rereading text that is reasonably easy for them—that is, text containing mostly words that they know or can decode easily." (3, p. 27)
Vocabulary Instruction in Guided Reading • Texts are selected so that students know most of the words but there are a few new words to provide opportunities for learning. • The teacher introduces the text to support comprehension, with specific attention to concepts and words. • Students read the text silently or orally with teacher support. • After reading, students and teacher discuss the meaning of the text, with further discussion of word meanings if needed. • The teacher teaches processing strategies, which may include both word recognition and how to determine word meanings. • Students may extend the meaning of the text through writing, which often includes attention to vocabulary. • The teacher provides 1–2 minutes of pre-planned word work which helps students attend to word parts and word meanings (affixes, word structure, homophones, synonyms, etc.).	"Extended instruction that promotes active engagement with vocabulary improves word learning." (3, p. 36) "Teaching specific words before reading helps both vocabulary learning and reading comprehension." (3, p. 36) "Repeated exposure to vocabulary in many contexts aids word learning." (3, p. 36) "Conversations about books help children to learn new words and concepts and to relate them to their prior knowledge and experience." (3, p. 35) "…the larger the reader's vocabulary (either oral or print), the easier it is to make sense of the text." (1, p. 13) "…children often hear adults repeat words several times. They also may hear adults use new and interesting words. The more oral language experiences children have, the more word meanings they learn." (3, p. 35)
Comprehension Instruction in Guided Reading • Teachers select texts that readers can process successfully with supportive teaching. • The teacher demonstrates effective strategies for comprehending text. • In the introduction to the text, the teacher explains words and concepts and assures that students activate their own prior knowledge. • Students have the opportunity to apply a range of strategies in response to the demands of texts.	"Comprehension is defined as 'intentional thinking during which meaning is constructed through interactions between text and reader' (Harris & Hodges, 1995). Thus, readers derive meaning from text when they engage in intentional, problem-solving thinking processes. The data suggest that text comprehension is enhanced when readers actively relate the ideas represented in print to their own knowledge and experiences and construct mental representations in memory." (1, p. 14) "In general, the evidence suggests that teaching a combination of reading comprehension techniques is the most effective. When students use them appropriately, they assist in recall, question answering, question generation, and summarization of texts. When used in combination, these techniques can improve results in standardized comprehension tests." (1, p. 15) "Text comprehension can be improved by instruction that helps readers use specific comprehension strategies." (2, p. 49)

• Students expand strategies by applying them, with teacher support, to texts that are more difficult than they could read independently. • Teachers help students extend their understandings through using oral language and writing. • Teachers help students extend their understanding through using graphic organizers to understand underlying text structures. • While teachers are working with students in small groups, other students read independently the books that they have previously read.	"Text comprehension can be improved by instruction that helps readers use specific comprehension strategies." (3, p. 9) "Graphic organizers illustrate concepts and interrelationships among concepts in a text, using diagrams or other pictorial devices. Regardless of the label, graphic organizers can help readers focus on concepts and how they are related to other concepts." "Comprehension strategies are not ends in themselves; they are means of helping your students understand what they are reading." (3, p. 6) "Help your students learn to use comprehension strategies in natural learning situations—for example, as they read in the content areas." (3, p. 65) "Readers must know what most of the words mean before they can understand what they are reading." (3, p. 45) "Children learn many new words by reading extensively on their own. The more children read on their own, the more words they encounter and the more word meanings they learn." (3, p. 35) "Teachers not only must have a firm grasp of the content presented in text, but also must have substantial knowledge of the strategies themselves, of which strategies are most effective for different students and types of content and of how best to teach and model strategy use." (1, p. 16)
Motivation Support in Guided Reading • Teachers select books that will be interesting to students. • Teachers introduce texts in a way that engages interest and motivation.	"Few if any studies have investigated the contribution of motivation to the effectiveness of phonics programs, not only the learner's motivation to learn but also the teacher's motivation to teach. The lack of attention to motivational factors by researchers in the design of phonics programs is potentially very serious … Future research should … be designed to determine which approaches teachers prefer to use and are most likely to use effectively in their classroom instruction." (2) "Interesting texts also provide mutual cognitive and motivational benefits (Schiefele, 1999). When students are interested in what they read, they process the material more deeply, gain richer conceptual understandings, and engage more fully with text." (4, p. 416)
Motivation Related to Reading Comprehension • Students who receive motivation support and strategy instruction improve their reading comprehension.	"Motivated students usually want to understand text content fully, and therefore, process information deeply. As they read frequently with these cognitive purposes, motivated students gain in reading proficiency. However, motivation and engagement have rarely been incorporated into experimental studies of instruction or interventions for reading comprehension." (4, p. 403) "(a) Engagement in reading refers to interaction with text that is simultaneously motivated and strategic, (b) engaged reading correlates with achievement in reading comprehension, (c) engaged reading and its constituents (motivation and cognitive strategies) can be increased by instruction practices directed toward them, and (d) an instructional framework that merges motivational and cognitive strategy support in reading will increase engaged reading and reading comprehension." (4, p. 403)

Effect of Engagement on Interest in Reading • Motivated readers are able to monitor their comprehension, recall what they read, and retain and organize the knowledge they gain. • Motivated readers are involved in their reading, often rereading and reflecting on their understanding. • Motivated readers know how reading is relevant to their lives. • Engaged readers find that reading is a meaningful, enjoyable activity.	"… the most highly interested students had positive affect toward books, favored certain authors, and enjoyed favorite topics. These high interest readers typically reread all or portions of books, pursued topics in and out of school, and connected reading to their personal experiences or feelings. Also salient was the students' deep comprehension and complex cognitive command of these texts that accompanied their enjoyment and enthusiasm. Students with high positive affect for a certain topic invariably had deep recollection of information or books about the topic, whereas students with low affect for reading on a topic displayed little recall and grasp of content. This suggests that high interest in reading is not limited to the strong, positive affect surrounding books, but also the high comprehension, recall, and organization of knowledge in memory typical of these readers." (5, p. 13)
Readers' Motivation to Be Responsible for Their Own Learning • Engaged readers are in control of their own learning and are able to express their opinions and their own understandings.	"A substantial proportion of students reported that knowledge and information was what they were seeking in books. We did not create this as a formal construct nor place it in our rubric, because we did not systematically ask all students about the extent that they read for knowledge. However, many students volunteered that they wanted to learn about their favorite topic, enjoyed gaining information, or liked being very well informed in certain domains. Being knowledgeable was an explicit goal mentioned by many, and while it is a common sense purpose for reading, it has not been formalized quantitatively in prior research as a motivational construct. We believe that reading for the purpose of knowledge development is a vitally important motivational attribute for future investigation." (5, p. 26)
Readers' Engagement With Text • For engaged readers, reading is a highly visual experience as they imagine characters, settings, and events. • Readers who are emotionally engaged in text can often note and understand ideas the author does not explicitly state. • Readers engage in an interchange of ideas between themselves and the text.	"… reading narrative text is often affectively laden, and that readers adopt affective goals for narrative reading. They seek excitement, emotional relationship with characters, interpersonal drama, and a range of aesthetic experiences. Reading information books, in contrast, is energized by goals of reading for knowledge, seeking information, and the desire to explain our physical or cultural worlds. Thus, motivations for reading narrative and information books should be distinguished in studying how motivation develops or how it relates to other factors such as reading comprehension." (5, pp. 26–27)
Features of Engaging Classrooms • Engaging classrooms are observational, conceptual, self-directed, strategic, collaborative, coherent, and personalized.	"To increase motivational development, teachers should provide support for situated experiences that increase intrinsic motivation. For example, an exciting activity that may be entertaining, such as reader's theater for a specific book, may increase situated, intrinsic motivation. Likewise, hands-on activities with science materials (a terrarium with plants and animals, or a field trip to a park) or hands-on activities in history (a reenactment of a historical scene within the classroom) will increase situated, intrinsic motivation for texts related to these topics. However, these events will be insufficient to influence long-term motivation for reading. Experimental evidence suggests that increasing generalized intrinsic motivation requires the extended classroom practices of support for students' choices, collaborations, use of interesting texts, and real-world interactions related to literacy." (6, p. 21)

The ideas in this chart are referenced to the following documents:

(1) National Institute of Child Health and Human Development. (2001). *Report of the National Reading Panel: Teaching children to read: An evidence-based assessment of the scientific research literature on reading and its implications for reading instruction.* Washington, DC: National Institutes of Health.

(2) National Institute of Child Health and Human Development. (2001). *Report of the National Reading Panel: Teaching children to read: An evidence-based assessment of the scientific research literature on reading and its implications for reading instruction: Report of the subgroups.* Washington, DC: National Institutes of Health.

(3) Armbruster, B. B., Lehr, F., & Osborn, J. (2001). *Put reading first: The research building blocks for teaching children to read, kindergarten through grade 3.* Washington, DC: U.S. Department of Education.

[i] "Readers must know what most of the words mean before they can understand what they are reading." (*Put Reading First*, p. 45)

[ii] "Beginning readers use their oral vocabulary to make sense of the words they see in print ... Readers must know what most of the words mean before they can understand what they are reading." (*Put Reading First*, p. 45)

(4) Guthrie, J. T., Wigfield, A., Barbosa, P., et al., (2004). Increasing reading comprehension and engagement through concept oriented reading instruction. *Journal of Educational Psychology, 96*(3), 403–423.

(5) Guthrie, J. T., Hoa, L. W., Wigfield, A., Tonks, S. M., Humenick, N. M., & Littles, E. (2007). Reading motivation and reading comprehension growth in the later elementary years. *Contemporary Educational Psychology, 32,* 282–313.

(6) Guthrie, J. T., Hoa, L. W., Wigfield, A., Tonks, S. M., & Perencevich, K. C. (2006). From spark to fire: Can situational reading interest lead to long-term reading motivation? *Reading Research and Instruction, 45*(2), 91–117.

BIBLIOGRAPHY

Allington, R. L. (2009). *What really matters in response to intervention*. New York: Addison-Wesley Longman.

Anderson, E., & Guthrie, J. T. (1999, April). *Motivating children to gain conceptual knowledge from text: The combination of science observation and interesting texts*. Paper presented at the annual meeting of the American Educational Research Association, Montreal, Canada.

Atwell, N. (2008). *The reading zone: How to help kids become skilled, passionate, habitual, critical readers*. New York, NY: Scholastic.

Biancarosa, G., Bryk, A., & Dexter, E. (2009). Assessing the value-added effects of coaching on student learning. Final report to the Institute of Education Sciences (IES).

Blevins, W., & Boynton, A. 5 keys to reading nonfiction. *The Art of Teaching*. Supplement to *Instructor Magazine*, 4–7.

Bolter, J. D. (2001). *Writing space: Computers, hypertext, and the remediation of print*. Mahwah, NJ: Lawrence Erlbaum Associates.

Box, J., et al. (2009). *The mile guide: Milestones for improving learning & education*. Tucson, AZ: The Partnership for 21st Century Skills.

Braunger, J., & Lewis, J. (2008). What we know about the learning and development of reading K–12: Thirteen core understandings about reading and learning to read. *What research really says about teaching and learning to read*. Edited by S. Kucer. Urbana, IL: National Council of Teachers of English.

Brown, H., & Cambourne, B. (1987). *Read and retell: A strategy for the whole-language/natural learning classroom*. Portsmouth, NH: Heinemann.

Burke, J. (2000). *Reading reminders: Tools, tips, and techniques*. Portsmouth, NH: Heinemann.

Caswell, L. J., & Duke, N. K. (1998). Non-narratives as a catalyst for literacy development. *Language Arts, 75*, 108–117.

Chall, J. S. (1983). *Stages of reading development*. New York, NY: McGraw-Hill.

Clay, M. M. (1993). *Reading recovery: A guidebook for teachers in training*. Portsmouth, NH: Heinemann.

Common core state standards for English language arts & literacy in history/social studies, science, and technical subjects (2010). Washington, DC: Common Core Standards Initiative.

Cortese, A., & Ravitch, D. (2008). Preface in *Still at risk: What students don't know, even now*. Washington, DC: Common Core.

Darling-Hammond, L. (2010). *The flat world and education: How America's commitment to equity will determine our future*. New York, NY: Teacher's College Press.

Dreher, M. J. (2000). Fostering reading for learning. In L. Baker, M. J. Dreher, & J. Guthrie (Eds.), *Engaging young readers: Promoting achievement and motivation* (pp. 94–118). New York, NY: Guilford.

Duke, N. K. (2000). 3.6 minutes per day: The scarcity of informational texts in first grade. *Reading Research Quarterly, 35*, 202–224.

Duke, N. K. (2003). Reading to learn from the very beginning: Information books in early childhood. *Young Children, 58*(2), 14–20.

Duke, N. K., & Bennett-Armistead, V. S. (2003). *Reading & writing informational text in the primary grades: Research-based practices*. New York, NY: Scholastic Inc.

Duke, N. K., Bennett-Armistead, V. S., & Roberts, E. M. (2002). Incorporating information text in the primary grades. In C. Roller (Ed.), *Comprehensive reading instruction across grade levels* (pp. 40–54). Newark, DE: International Reading Association.

Duke, N. K., & Caughlan, S., Juzwik, M. M., Martin, N. M. (2011). *Reading & writing genre with purpose.* Portsmouth, NH: Heinemann.

Duke, N. K., & Kays, J. (1998). Can I say 'once upon a time'?: Kindergarten children developing knowledge of information book language. *Early Childhood Research Quarterly, 13,* 295-318.

Dymock, S. (2005). Teaching expository text structure awareness. *The Reading Teacher, 59*(2), 177-181.

Essential components of RTI—A closer look at response to intervention. (2010). Washington, DC: National Center on Response to Intervention. Retrieved from: http://www.rti4success.org/index.php?option=com_content&task=view&id=448&Itemid=93

Fountas, I., & Pinnell, G. S. (1996). *Guided reading: Good first teaching for all children.* Portsmouth, NH: Heinemann.

Fountas, I., & Pinnell, G. S. (Eds.). (1999). *Voices on word matters.* Portsmouth, NH: Heinemann.

Fountas, I., & Pinnell, G. S. (2001). *Guiding readers and writers, grades 3-6.* Portsmouth, NH: Heinemann.

Fountas, I., & Pinnell, G. S. (2006). *Teaching for comprehending and fluency: Thinking, talking, and writing about reading, K-8.* Portsmouth, NH: Heinemann.

Fountas, I., & Pinnell, G. S. (2009). *When readers struggle: Teaching that works.* Portsmouth, NH: Heinemann.

Gibson, A., Gold, J., & Sgouras, C. (2003, Spring). The power of story retelling. *The Tutor.*

Harris, T. L., & Hodges, R. E. (1995). *The literacy dictionary: The vocabulary of reading and writing.* Newark, DE: International Reading Association.

Hoffman, J. V., Roser, N. L., Salas, R., Patterson, E., & Pennington, J. (2000). *Text leveling and little books in first-grade reading* (CIERA Report No. 1-0). Ann Arbor, MI: Center for the Improvement of Early Reading Achievement, University of Michigan.

Jobe, R., & Dayton-Sakari, M. (2002). *Info-kids: How to use nonfiction to turn reluctant readers into enthusiastic learners.* Markham, Ontario, Canada: Pembroke.

Johnston, P. (2010). An instructional frame for RTI. *The Reading Teacher, 63*(7), 602-604.

Johnston, P. (In Press). Response to intervention in literacy: Problems and possibilities. *Elementary School Journal, 11*(4), 511-534.

Kamil, M. L., & Lane, D. M. (1998). Researching the relation between technology and literacy: An agenda for the 21st century. In D. R. Reinking, L. D. Labbo, M. McKenna, & R. Kieffer (Eds.), *Literacy for the 21st century: Technological transformations in a post-typographic world* (pp. 235-251). Mahwah, NJ: Lawrence Erlbaum Associates.

Kucer, S. B. (Ed.). (2008). *What research really says about teaching and learning to read.* Urbana, IL: National Council of Teachers of English.

National Governors Association Center for Best Practices, Council of Chief State School Officers. (2010). *Common Core State Standards for English language arts and literacy in history/social studies, science, and technical subjects.* Washington, DC: Author.

Partnership for 21st Century Skills. (2009). *The Mile Guide: Milestones for improving learning & education.* Tucson, AZ: Author.

Pinnell, G. S., & Fountas, I. C. (1999). *Matching books to readers: A leveled book list for guided reading, K-3.* Portsmouth, NH: Heinemann.

Pinnell, G. S., & Fountas, I. C. (1998). *Word matters: Teaching phonics and spelling in the reading/writing classroom.* Portsmouth, NH: Heinemann.

Pinnell, G. S., Pikulski, J. J., Wixson, K. K., Campbell, J. R., Gough, R. B., & Beatty, A. S. (1995). *Listening to children read aloud: Data from NAEP's Integrated Reading Performance Record (IRPR) at grade 4.* (Report No. 23-FR-04). Prepared by Educational Testing Service under contract with the National Center for Education Statistics, Office of Educational Research and Improvement, U.S. Department of Education.

Reading framework for the 2009 National Assessment of Educational Progress. (2009). National Assessment Governing Board. Washington, DC. Retrieved from: http://www.nagb.org/publications/frameworks/reading09.pdf

Reading framework for the 2011 National Assessment of Educational Progress. (2011). National Assessment Governing Board. Washington, DC. Retrieved from: http://www.nagb.org/assets/documents/publications/frameworks/reading-2011-framework.pdf

Resnick, L. (1987, December). The 1987 presidential address: Learning in school and out. *Educational Researcher, 16*(9), 13–54.

Schiefele, U. (1999). Interest and learning from text. *Scientific Studies of Reading, 3,* 257–280.

Schulman, M., & Payne, C. (2000). *Guided reading: Making it work: Two teachers share their insights, strategies, and lessons for helping every child become a successful reader.* New York, NY: Scholastic Inc.

Smith, M.C. (2000). The real-world reading practices of adults. *Journal of Literacy Research, 32*(1), 25–52. doi:10.1080/10862960009548063

Taylor, B. M., Pearson, P. D., Clark, K., & Walpole, S. (2000). Effective schools and accomplished teachers: Lessons about primary grade reading instruction in low income schools. *Elementary School Journal, 101*(2), 121–165.

Trilling, B., & Fadel, C. (2009). *21st century skills: Learning for life in our times.* San Francisco, CA: Jossey-Bass.

Venezky, R. L. (1982). The origins of the present-day chasm between adult literacy needs and school literacy instruction. *Visible Language, 16,* 112–127.

Wilson, P. T., & Anderson, R. C. (1986). What they don't know will hurt them: The role of prior knowledge in comprehension. In J. Orasanu (Ed.), *Reading comprehension: From research to practice* (pp. 31–48). Hillsdale, NJ: LEA.

RESEARCH AND VALIDATION

A strong pattern of rising scores has been found in schools where daily guided reading has been combined with phonics and word study mini-lessons and daily writing workshops. For further information, see:

Scharer, P., Williams, E. J., & Pinnell, G. S. (2001). *Literacy collaborative 2001 research report.* Columbus, OH: The Ohio State University.

Williams, E. J., Scharer, P., & Pinnell, G. S. (2000). *Literacy collaborative 2002 research report.* Columbus, OH: The Ohio State University.

Williams, J. (2002). The power of data utilization in bringing about systemic school change. *Mid-Western Educational Researcher, 15,* 4–10.

NOTES

NOTES